Out of the Cobra's Clutches

To. Hank and Diane
you will enjoy reading about
"our India"

Allen Buchwalter

Out of the Cobra's Clutches

by Thangam
as told to Allen Buckwalter

Evangel
Press

301 N. Elm St.
Nappanee, Indiana 46550

Cover design and illustrations: Weston Phipps

ISBN: 0-916035-17-4

Printed in the United States of America

Contents

Introduction

Speak of India, and it conjures up pictures of tigers and peacocks, snake charmers and holy men, Hindu mystics, high caste Brahmans, and lowly untouchables.

Leoda and I entered this India as missionaries in 1939. But the gospel preceded us by nearly two thousand years! The Apostle Thomas established a church in the extreme southern part of the sub-continent during the first century. Even today, a vibrant body proudly bears his name—Mar Thoma (Son of Thomas).

A small colony of Jews still exists in South India. It possesses written records of its settlement which date back to the fourth century.

The modern missionary movement began about the time of the conquest of India by the British. Consequently, Christianity and the British government, still called "the British Raj," became confused in the thinking of the Indians. Despised as following a foreign religion, new converts met harsh treatment and sometimes death. They had forfeited their position in the strong Hindu society. Yet their diligence and character often won them grudging respect and a higher economic living status.

Ratnam was born into such a society in the 19th century. He turned to Christianity from the Brahman priesthood. His granddaughter, Thangam, shared his story with us. It needs to be retold. It reveals village life—the struggles, the anguish, the rejection—and Ratnam's final triumph.

I now share Ratnam's story with you. My special thanks to my wife, Leoda, for her hours of editing the manuscript, and to Virginia Weaver, who aided her.

—Allen Buckwalter
Elizabethtown, Pennsylvania

Glossary

Amma—proper name, as Mama

amma—madam; when used in direct address, it means "respected mother"

Appa—proper name, as Papa

appa—gentleman, when used in direct address, it means "sir" or "father"

caste—a Hindu group united by its social position; i.e. Brahmans are the highest caste, while outcastes are untouchables

lungi—cloth skirt worn in South India by men, reaching from waist to ground; usually white for festive occasions, otherwise colored

mantra—incantations, chanted by Hindu priests

pan—(pronounced pahn) A digestive aid, often taken following meals; made of betel nut leaves with other ingredients rolled in the leaf; the juice is red, like blood

Raj—literally, kingdom or rule; the British Raj is a general term used for the British rule and authority over India; *Swaraj* means ruling oneself, and is used currently for homerule

rupee—monetary unit of India

sari—national garb for ladies in India—a cloth 5½—6 yards long and 48 inches wide, tastefully tied, with some variations in different parts of the country

Swamiji—religious teacher

Tamil—one of the languages of southern India

Vedas—ancient Hindu Scriptures, dating back to the time of Abraham

Chapter One
Priest Confronts Priest

Ratnam, the village priest, paused in his chanting of the Vedic scriptures and stood up uncertainly. He tightened the loose-fitting cotton skirt around his tall frame and sighed. It was a hot day. The sacred cord, denoting his Brahman lineage and position, clung to his half-naked body.

The priest squinted skyward to note the sun's position. It was time to feed the cobra, sacred deity of the local area. Ratnam took a gold platter from the shelf inside the temple door. He set it on a mat in front of the shrine. Then he poured it full of fresh milk. Taking another platter, the priest banged it against the temple to start vibrations which would move the sluggish reptile from its coiled position on the mud floor.

The cobra slithered toward the platter, and the priest bowed low in obeisance.

This ritual completed, the priest waved the creature back into the inner recesses of the temple and again began chanting the *mantras.*

Ratnam usually enjoyed reciting the ancient wisdom of the Vedas, but today his chants sounded mechanical. A disturbing sound came from the village. He couldn't concentrate, so he listened. Yes, there it was again. A song? He seemed to hear several voices singing.

Curious to see what was happening, the priest stopped his worship and moved toward the marketplace in the heart of the village. As he neared the edge of the crowd, he heard someone speaking in Tamil, but with a slight accent. He caught a few phrases: "The Lord Jesus died . . . your sins . . . a cross . . . rose from the grave . . . alive and now your priest. . . ."

Disbelief and anger shook the spiritual head of this Hindu community. "Who dares take my place?" he shouted as he neared the group in the center. "I'm the priest in this village! Challenge me, if you please. I'll show you who's priest here."

The crowd parted to let him through. His attention focused on a white man dressed in Indian shirt and *lungi.* His three companions, Indians, apparently were his friends. Ratnam's neighbors stood apart, listening warily.

Again Ratnam shouted, "Who are you, and what are you talking about? Priest?" he stormed. "I'm the only priest in this village, I'll have you know. And I'll not suffer any interference!"

His inflammatory tone normally would have produced an angry reply, but the speaker turned to Ratnam with a placid face and shining blue eyes.

"Brother," he said, "I, too, am a priest—a priest of the most high God. He is the creator and ruler of us all."

"Ruler?" Ratnam stopped, confused. "Do you mean the British Raj?"

"Oh, no," came the gentle reply. "No, this one is Lord of the British rulers, as well as all others. May I tell you about Him?"

Ratnam shook his head so violently that the little knot of hair at the nape of his neck unfastened. Retying it hastily, he retorted, "No, no! I don't want any nonsense. You'd better leave this village or there'll be trouble."

The white man smiled and said, "Brother, God loves you, and he desires to do something special for you." The foreigner continued, "I have just moved into the last house on the road, opposite the pond. I'd be glad to have you come and visit me soon."

Shocked at the very thought of visiting an outcaste, Ratnam shook his head so vigorously his hair came loose again. The priest turned abruptly and strode back to the temple. He could feel the curious stares of his people, and this upset him. Too angry to continue his *mantras*, the priest retied his hair, finished some odd jobs around the temple, and returned home.

Chapter Two

The Agitated Priest

Ratnam always found consolation at home with his beautiful wife Padmini and his two sons, aged seven and three. As he neared the house, Raju, the seven-year-old, ran out to meet him. Ratnam greeted him fondly, tousling his hair, and hoisted him to his shoulder. Together, they entered to Padmini's loving greeting. Ratnam put the lad down, then went into the inner courtyard to wash.

Meanwhile, Padmini brought his meal and sat nearby to serve him. His anger had stolen his appetite, but he didn't have the heart to disappoint his wife. After a few flattering remarks about her delicious cooking, the priest hurriedly finished his meal and retired to his room.

Ratnam rolled out the thick mat on the floor and lay down. He soon felt Raju snuggling close. This was routine. The priest patted his son lovingly. Half-listening to Raju's happy chatter, he suddenly came to full attention.

"*Appa*, there's a white lady living near the pond," Raju reported with excitement. "She tries to talk Tamil, but sometimes she makes mistakes which sound funny. We laugh, and she laughs with us. I like her. So do the other boys. She tells us stories. Even though her Tamil is queer, we help her, and then we all laugh. She asked us back tomorrow." He added wistfully, "*Appa*, may I go?"

Ratnam tried to control his voice, "It's time to sleep now, Raju," he replied gently. "We'll see tomorrow."

Satisfied, the boy slept.

Ratnam stretched himself and let his mind wander over the happenings of the past few hours. He had been severely shaken and he needed to reflect on his encounter with the white man.

4

Now this, from Raju. She must be his wife, thought the priest.

"Brother!" The word rang in his ears. Brother? Shocking! How can an Indian be brother to a white man? Never! But this Britisher said it with love. Over and over again Ratnam heard his words, "I, too, am a priest—of the one, true God."

Throughout the years, Ratnam had enjoyed the prestige of his priestly office. Now he resented interference. Why should this man come to challenge his spiritual leadership in the village?

Padmini entered quietly and lay on a mat close to her husband. She sensed his restlessness, but decided against questioning him. Tired from her day's work, she soon dropped off to sleep.

The atmosphere in the small room seemed hot and oppressive to Ratnam. Longing for fresh air, he quickly rose and stole out of the house. The cool breeze refreshed him as he walked aimlessly through the village.

It was a moonlit night. Ratnam suddenly realized he had come to the pond. He might as well see where these white people live. The village was asleep. No harm could possibly come from his investigation. Funny, he thought, I didn't know about them before today. Of course the white man said they just arrived, and this is the other end of the village from our home.

The priest found the house, set apart from the others, but in most respects like the rest. Ratnam chuckled to himself, "Foreign outcastes! Paying doubly high rent, I'll wager."

While all the other dwellings were dark, a bright light shone from the one at the end of the road. Ratnam crept toward an open window. He raised himself and quickly scanned the room. Inside he saw a few wooden boxes, several books lying on one. In the center of the room a small table held a large lantern, and kneeling in its light, with hands folded in the gesture of prayer, were the white man and his wife.

He appeared to be talking to someone nearby, yet Ratnam could see nobody else. It made the village priest uneasy. What sort of magic was this? Were they reciting *mantras*? He'd better leave before they cast a spell on him. After another furtive glance Ratnam, the village priest, cautiously moved from the house and returned home, more perplexed and uncertain than ever.

Chapter Three
The Challenge

Next morning, Raju came running to greet him. "*Appa, Appa,*" he cried excitedly, "today is 'tomorrow.' Remember? You said you would see tomorrow."

Baffled, Ratnam looked at Raju, then remembered all that had happened yesterday. The confrontation in the market, his boy's story about the white woman, and the late night visit to the white man's house all flashed through the priest's mind.

"Tell me, *Appa,*" insisted the little voice, breaking his father's reverie. "May I go to the white woman's house today?"

Ratnam shouted, "No! The white people do *mantras,* and I don't want any harm to come to you."

"That's not true!" Bursting into sobs, Raju fled and buried

his tear-stained face in the folds of his mother's *sari*. Padmini threw her husband a reproachful glance, then tried to appease the unhappy lad while Ratnam hurriedly ate breakfast and left for duties at the temple.

The village priest lit the lamps, offered curds and flowers to the cobra, and fed him. But Ratnam worked automatically throughout the day, his mind in turmoil. And that night he tossed and turned, too upset to realize that Raju had avoided him. He didn't know yet that for the first time his son had disobeyed him and returned to visit the "white *amma*."

Raju's mother had listened sympathetically to her son's confidence, hiding it in her heart. "She told us such wonderful stories, *Amma*," he had told his mother. "She forgot the Tamil words and we helped her. Then we all laughed. We played games outside, too. It was fun."

Some days later, Raju brought home a slate and pencil and proudly showed his mother how to write the letters he had learned from the white *amma*. Padmini felt excited at her son's new accomplishment. She couldn't understand her husband's moodiness and irritation.

Now the village began to seethe with rumors. One evening the elders visited Ratnam. They informed him that the white couple, helped by two Tamilians, were teaching about a new god. Their children, in particular, seemed to be greatly influenced by the white *amma*.

Suddenly Ratnam realized his son had been avoiding him. Was Raju also visiting that house? With great effort, the priest listened to the allegations of the group against the newcomers. During a lull, Ratnam spoke, "Why don't you do something about it?"

"But you are our religious leader," they countered. "You should order them to leave the village. It's your job, not ours."

Ratnam hesitated, then nodded assent. "Well, yes, I'll do it."

"Should one of us go with you?" they asked.

"No!" the priest replied indignantly. Did they consider him incapable? He added grimly, "If I fail, I'll let you know." He concluded tersely, "Meet me here tomorrow night," and dismissed the group.

Troubled at the implications of again facing the white man,

the priest decided to consult his wife. In the past he had found her to be a good sounding board, and after this period of troubled silence, he knew it was past time to talk things over. After the evening meal, Padmini put the children to bed, then sat down beside her husband.

As he talked, she merely listened. At times, he seemed embarrassed, then again he would chuckle. He finally climaxed his story with the demands of the village elders.

"It's too much," Ratnam concluded with a sigh, "but I agree something has to be done. The elders say it's my responsibility. I sometimes feel they're using me to do a job they don't want to tackle."

Padmini spoke up, "But why should you tell the white people to leave? They're not robbers or thieves! They're good! Be careful of what you say to them. And look at what they've done for Raju and me."

She stopped abruptly, aware he didn't know of his family's friendship with the newcomers. Then she continued slowly, "Please don't be angry with us, Ratnam. Raju has been attending the white *amma's* school. I allowed him to go."

"What?" The man looked at his wife in amazement. "And you never told me?" he shouted.

"Hush," she said, laying a restraining hand on her husband's arm. "The children are sleeping."

She continued quietly, "You seemed so worried, so preoccupied with other things. I just kept quiet. I'm sorry—but look at this!" Padmini brought the slate with the lesson that Raju had just taught her. She spelled the words out shyly and confessed, "See, Ratnam, Raju's teaching me to read."

He noted her obvious pride and wondered what to say. True, Raju had disobeyed his father's command, but Padmini allowed it. Now, both mother and son were learning to read, an obvious accomplishment! Pride suddenly welled up inside the priest, and he felt ashamed for the way he had reacted before. Clearly, the white man's *mantras* hadn't harmed his family!

For some reason, the whole incident suddenly appeared ludicrous, and the village priest began to chuckle.

Chapter Four

The Interview

Next morning Ratnam lingered in the house. He seemed to be waiting for something. Raju noticed it and felt uncomfortable. Why was his father still at home? Then he saw the big smile on his face and those arms outstretched to receive him as before. Raju ran to his father and jumped up.

"Son," he heard his father say, "I'm sorry I roared at you like a big, bad tiger. Remember when? Yes, and I found out you're going to the white *amma*. But don't worry. You may go! Now, are we friends?"

The boy gave him a big hug, then shouted, "*Amma! Amma!* It's all right. *Appa* says I may go!"

Padmini's heart swelled with pride and joy. Her men had made peace.

Ratnam patted his son on the head. Then he left the house, a new song within. He hurried through his morning duties at the temple, then turned southward. Somewhere along the way, he lost the song; the old uneasiness took over. Added to the troublesome job of again facing the white man was the fact that he was a Brahman, and the white people were foreigners—untouchables! He dare not step inside that house!

The white man came to the door. "Good morning, brother," he said as Ratnam turned up the path. "I've been expecting you."

"Expecting me?" questioned the priest. "But I didn't send a message. Did someone give you advance word?"

"No, no, not that. I'll tell you later."

"Sir," replied Ratnam, "could we talk together somewhere?"

"Why, yes," the foreigner replied. "I'd enjoy welcoming you to my home, but I know how you feel. Perhaps the pond is a better place. Come, let's sit in the shade of that mango tree."

9

Ratnam gratefully nodded his assent as they crossed the field to the overspreading tree beside the pond. Each found a clean spot on which to sit, then fell silent with their thoughts.

The Englishman sensed Ratnam's embarrassment. "What is it, brother?" he prompted. "You don't need to fear."

The priest cleared his throat. Padmini's words, "They're good people," floated before him, as did the anger of the village elders. He began to speak hesitantly.

"Please, sir, the elders have delegated me to come to you. They're very angry and they want you to leave immediately. You must stop your teaching or there will be trouble. If you stay, sir, they may attack you. I advise you to go at once."

Relieved to have conveyed the message, Ratnam waited.

The Englishman sat silently, hands clasped around his knees. As he continued to gaze into the distance, his companion shifted uneasily. Somehow Ratnam felt drawn to this foreigner who had done him no wrong. With an impulsive gesture, Ratnam reached out and touched the stranger. "I don't feel angry with you," he said quietly, "and I won't do anything to harm you. But I can't guarantee the behavior of others. Some are fanatics, and evil."

The man turned to Ratnam. "Thank you for coming, brother, and thank you for listening to me. I can't do what your people request," he said earnestly. "My God sent me here. I can't leave! But I know He will take care of me, regardless of what happens. You see, my brother, if you love people, you desire to share good things with them. Isn't that right?"

Ratnam nodded, although he didn't understand. His companion continued, "The God I worship doesn't live in earthly temples, nor in idols. He's the true and living God. We know Him, and love Him. He puts love within our hearts," continued the Englishman, "and that's why we love others, even our enemies."

Ratnam winced, but said nothing.

"He speaks to me and my wife through His written word, the Holy Bible. And He has sent us to preach good news. That's why we're here. We must obey our God." The man looked directly at the Hindu priest, and added firmly, "Please believe me, brother, we really desire to help. We want to bless you and your people. Your children are learning to read and write. Isn't that a good thing?" He paused, waiting thoughtfully.

Words and ideas tumbled through Ratnam's mind: the living God—no temple—no idols or *pujas*—the cobra—representing ignorance, darkness! What did it all mean?

The priest felt himself sinking, and with an effort he pulled his thoughts together. "I'm sorry," he said simply. "I've done what the elders told me to do. The outcome is in the hands of others. I must go now."

Ratnam could not trust his emotions. He rose swiftly and strode away before the Englishman had a chance to reply. His mind in turmoil, he wanted to talk to someone. Padmini? Yes, she would understand! He turned toward home.

His wife listened patiently.

"I found it impossible to speak harshly to him," he confided.

"Those white people are good." she replied earnestly. "Don't feel anxious about them. And listen to this!" She smiled broadly, then divulged her secret. "I talked today to that little boy who used to sit in the market begging. Remember him?"

Ratnam nodded, watching his wife's vivid features.

"Well," she continued, "the white lady has taken him to her

house, Ratnam! Would you believe it? She's cut his matted hair, bathed him, and dressed him in clean clothes. He told me all about it when I met him this morning. You should see how happy he is! And," she exclaimed triumphantly, "he said his white *amma* gave him a whole *rupee* to buy fruit and vegetables. You should have heard him bargain with the shopkeepers! He's smart, you know! He made them give him produce—at the right price!" Padmini laughed aloud.

"That's not all," she continued. "I watched Arputham— that's his name—when some men started teasing him. He refused to fight back and said his *amma* told him not to answer. He just walked off. The funny thing is the men almost came to blows between themselves. Plenty of our people like the foreigners. No, Ratnam, you're not alone!"

Chapter Five

Ratnam Reports

The village elders arrived earlier than expected. They settled themselves noisily on the narrow verandah. Manickam and his good friend, Dassan, vigorously chewed some *betel* nut and loudly inhaled their snuff.

Ratnam, seeing them through the open door, suspected these two of planning the expulsion of the foreigners. As the priest passed his wife, he motioned in their direction and muttered, "Vultures! Hypocrites! No good themselves, nor do they desire anything good around them."

The priest stepped onto the verandah, carefully closing the door behind him. His mind whirled: "That fat Manickam! Look at him . . . smug, pious, deceitful! I'm sure he robbed the money box in the temple when I went to District Headquarters. And that loathsome friend of his, Dassan! They make me sick. . . ."

He quickly brushed these thoughts aside, however, as he turned to the men. Puturaj he liked, sensing him to be honest, as were Siromani and some of the others. But where was Appu, the storekeeper? Ratnam and Appu had been friends for years. Why hadn't he come?

Sitting on a stool near the door, the priest cleared his throat to gain attention. He then described the interview in detail, recounting the white man's refusal to leave the village. His listeners murmured their disbelief and disapproval. But Ratnam continued to speak, mentioning Arputham, and the school where the village children were gaining reading skills.

"I know that to be a fact," broke in Puturaj. "Why should we desire to drive these people from our midst? They're doing us good!"

"Nonsense!" growled Manickam, spitting a stream of red *betel* juice into the dusty street. "Who wants their good? They'll just expect us to accept their religion, too." He paused for effect. "Just watch! We'll have all sorts of trouble if they stay. You'll remember my words!"

"I agree!" shouted Dassan. In his excitement he almost fell from the verandah, and Ratnam tried to suppress a smile.

"Why not take the good they're doing?" proposed the priest. "We can leave them in peace with their God. They're not ordering us around like the British Raj, are they? It seems to me they're quiet, decent people."

Manickam looked at Ratnam disdainfully. "Has the white man cast his spell on you?" he sneered. "Or maybe his wife has been giving gifts to your son?"

Ratnam stood up, towering over the group. His words cut like a knife as he retorted angrily, "Manickam, shut up! I'm finished with you and your scheming! Goodnight, gentlemen. The matter is yours to handle."

The priest nodded and went inside, closing the door behind him.

"So?" Manickam grinned widely, even while his exclamation fell upon the stunned group as a pebble in a pond. He rose, stretched, and observed, "Well, we're on our own, are we? Our respected, spiritual leader got offended, did he? Come on, Dassan, we have more important work to do than to sit here."

Puturaj, elderly and wizened, watched them intently as they left. Then turning to his companions he commented, "I'd say Manickam and Dassan are on their own! I cast my vote with Ratnam."

"Here, too," said Siromani. The remaining three elders nodded as he added, "Puturaj, you and I have lived longer than that rich moneylender Manickam. Perhaps we have learned more!"

"I'd say trouble is brewing," added another. "We'd better stay alert."

Clearly, the matter of the foreigners remained a controversial issue, even though the meeting had adjourned.

———

Ratnam busied himself with routine duties in the temple for

several days, then went to District Headquarters on business. Returning the next day on foot, he noted a group of people standing near the market. All seemed quiet enough. Coming closer, he recognized the Englishman as the speaker, holding the attention of his neighbors. Suddenly Dassan, followed by two men, rushed through the crowd and brandished heavy sticks in the white man's face. They grabbed his book and flung it into the dust. In the shuffle which followed, they tore the preacher's shirt and beat him. A blow on his head felled him, unconscious, to the ground.

Too stunned to act, the crowd watched. Some wanted to help, but all feared Dassan. Who among them had courage to face Dassan? They knew him to be the leader of a gang of thugs, hired by Manickam, the rich moneylender. Already heavily in debt, most of the villagers felt like Manickam's pawns.

Not so with Ratnam!

Seeing the commotion, he ran and forced his way through the crowd. Reaching the center of action, Ratnam shouted in anger, "How dare you do such a dastardly thing to anyone?" The thugs cowered before him.

"There, take that!" He knocked one down and pushed the other away. Fearing for their lives, the men disappeared.

Ratnam fell to his knees beside the unconscious figure. Most of the onlookers melted away to a safer distance, not ready to become involved. "We'll be in trouble if this man dies," they whispered to each other in fear and added, "He's an Englishman!"

"Bring me some water," Ratnam cried.

"Here, take this," said Puturaj from his front verandah. He pushed a brass vessel into a boy's hand. The lad quickly filled it at the pump and carried it to the priest. Ratnam wet the end of his cotton cloth and wiped the dirt and blood from the fair hands and face of the stricken man. He shouted for a cot, but this time there was no response. Puturaj had gone around to the back of his house. The other onlookers suddenly realized that their Brahman priest was kneeling beside an untouchable. Ratnam shouted again, "Hurry! If this man dies. . . ."

At that moment Puturaj returned. "A cot? Yes, here's a bamboo one." He signaled several outcastes watching from a distance.

Four came a bit reluctantly, but Puturaj said, "Take it quickly, men. I'll pay you when you return."

The leader nodded, and the bearers moved to Ratnam and lifted the patient onto the stretcher. Ratnam picked up the Bible, wiped off the dust and placed it beside the white man. With the priest leading, the party moved toward the house at the end of the village.

Chapter Six

With the Untouchables

News of the assault and rescue had already reached the white *amma*, and she awaited them on the verandah. One look at the limp figure of her husband caused her to blanch in fear, but the tall, fair Indian beside him said softly, "He's alive. He'll be all right."

Even as the bearers placed the cot inside the house, the man stirred. His wife kneeled quickly and said, "Peter! Peter! It's Mary. I'm with you here in our own home. You'll be all right soon."

He opened his eyes and smiled. Embarrassed, the outcastes slipped out, taking time, however, to glance at the furnishings of these foreigners.

Ratnam stood by. He felt a strange attachment to this man whom his people had mistreated. The white woman, recognizing him as the priest, spoke softly, "*Swamiji*, I've heard about you from my husband and your son, Raju. What can I do for you and those kind men outside? It's so good of you to help my husband. Will they take money?"

"No, no, *amma*," objected Ratnam. "They will go now."

He went out and told the men they could leave, but the white *amma* called from within, asking them to wait. She quickly brought a basket of fruit and gave it to them.

"Divide this," she said with a smile. "And thank you for bringing my husband home. I'll never forget your kindness."

Long after the others left, Ratnam lingered. He helped *amma* to apply medicines to the cuts and bruises. Then she brought a glass of cool milk which the tired man drank eagerly.

Suddenly the young Arputham ran into the room. "*Amma, Amma*," he sobbed, "what has happened? They tried to kill him!"

17

He flung himself down by the bed and cried, "Those wicked, wicked men! Just wait. . . . I'll. . . ." His voice trailed off as he blubbered. Then he felt Peter's hand on his head. "Wait a minute, Arputham," said Peter soothingly. "This is no way to behave. We must not be angry. Remember the Lord Jesus? He wants us to love our enemies, and do good to those who hate us. I'll be all right soon. Run along now and finish your work."

The boy slowly wiped his tear-stained face and left the room. Peter looked up at Ratnam. "You've been standing a long time. Sit down, brother."

The man continued standing and the Englishman asked, "How can I thank you for what you have done?"

No answer.

"I guess this won't make you very popular in the village, will it?"

Ratnam hung his head, remembering the insults thrown at him as he accompanied the stricken man on the cot. He said nothing, but Peter spoke softly, "I would like to help you in any way possible."

Ratnam grunted an embarrassed acknowledgement and shifted uneasily as the white *amma* settled comfortably on a wooden box nearby. Peter reached out and touched Ratnam's arm and began to talk.

"My name is Peter, and *amma* is my wife, Mary. We have come from the land of the British Raj."

The priest nodded, and Peter continued slowly. "We are Christians, as you know. We aren't associated with the government, but rather with the Lord Jesus Christ." He paused, wincing as he tried to turn on the cot. Mary and Ratnam quickly helped, and after retaking their places, Peter continued. "Thank you, *Swamiji*, I feel much more comfortable now. As I was saying, it's our desire to help you and your people to know the true and living God. We can teach your children and treat your illnesses. Isn't that good?"

The priest nodded again. Since Ratnam seemed in no hurry to leave, Peter recounted the story of redemption slowly and carefully. Mary added her personal testimony.

"*Swamiji*," she said, "I have peace in my heart since I believed on Jesus. He's changed my life, and given me His love. I had a wicked temper before, but now . . ." she smiled, then continued, "now the Lord has given me love for everybody, . . . even those who hurt my husband."

The priest rose from his seat. Bowing slightly, with hands folded, he said, "I have learned much today. Please, may I leave now? But . . ." he paused, then added, "I hope you will allow me to return. I'd like to hear more."

In a moment, Ratnam had gone.

Chapter Seven
Confrontation

"Raju, Raju," called his friend, Ram. "See? Something's happening in the marketplace. Come!"

The two boys had sprinted down the road on their return from the white woman's house where sounds of commotion led them. They had arrived just in time for Raju to see his father stride into the group and fling aside several men with sticks.

Raju fled home. Tears rolling down his cheeks, he sobbed, "*Amma*! I don't know what's happened to the white man, but he's lying on the ground with blood on his face. In the marketplace, *Amma*! And *Appa* came just in time to chase two men with sticks away. Oh, *Amma*, will the white *appa* die?"

Padmini held her son close, trying to comfort him. Her mind started piecing the puzzle together. Somebody had assaulted the foreigner with sticks? He was unconscious? Her husband rushed to the rescue? Now, what would that involvement mean?

There were times when Padmini resented the ties which caste bound about her, but she wasn't sure she wanted to be considered an outcaste because of her husband's hasty action. Yet, she countered, would any good come of obeying caste rules when the life of a man was at stake? She shuddered, then threw her shoulders back. Whatever price this involvement with the European would cost Ratnam, she was ready to bear it with him. Padmini drew Raju closer, wondering what price her son also might have to pay.

It wasn't long until Raju learned. Ram, his closest friend, walked on the opposite side of the road when Raju called out a half-hour later, "Come, Ram, tell me what happened."

"I can't, Raju," the boy replied forlornly. "My father says I'm not to talk to you anymore, and I can't go to the white *amma's* house either. Your father is an outcaste now! He's taken the white *appa* home."

Raju broke into tears, running indoors to his mother. Again he sheltered in the folds of her *sari* as he cried in frustration and grief. Again she held the boy close and soothed him, assuring him that *Appa* had done the right thing in helping the white man.

Then she concluded, "Raju, sometimes doing right brings good things; other times it might bring hard things to bear. *Appa* has done what he felt he should, and you and I are his family. We love him, don't we?"

The boy nodded, clinging tightly to his mother. Padmini continued, "When *Appa* comes home, he will be very tired. He has walked a long way today from headquarters and now has this to bear. So you'll be quiet, won't you? But just let him know you love him? Will you, Raju?"

"Yes, *Amma*." He squeezed her hard, adding, "And I love you, too."

Thoughts crowded Ratnam's mind as he walked slowly through the village on his return from Peter's house. Nobody greeted him. A feeling of loneliness engulfed the man, until Padmini met him at the door.

"Ratnam!" she cried, hands extended. "Are you . . . is he all right?" she stammered through her tears.

"Come," he said tenderly, "Where's Raju?"

"Playing in the back yard," she replied. "He saw you helping the white man and ran to tell me, then came again when Ram wouldn't talk with him because you're an outcaste."

The man shuddered, then looked his wife in the eyes. "Yes, Padmini, there will likely be a price to pay, but if I hadn't done it, Peter might have died."

"Peter?" she whispered. "Is that his name?"

"I have much to share with you, my dear. Do you want to talk?"

"Yes, yes, Ratnam. I don't care what other people say about you . . . I know you've done what you felt you should."

The priest squared his shoulders and straightened as though facing a challenge. He answered, "I needed that right now, Padmini. I sense I'm not alone?"

She smiled and replied softly, "Whatever this costs you,

Ratnam, I know you have saved the life of a good man, and I'm proud of you!"

Then, as they sat together, husband and wife shared the story of this memorable day's happenings.

Ratnam had just finished his evening meal when he heard a sound of shuffling feet and the loud clearing of throats announcing the arrival of visitors. He finished his coffee, took a deep breath, and went to the door. Nor was he surprised to find Manickam and Dassan sitting on the verandah, waiting for him. They looked more smug and crafty than ever, and Ratnam felt annoyance at having to meet them. It was as though they exulted in facing one who had just broken caste rules. Once again, Ratnam straightened to full height, then walked out to meet their challenge.

With a brief nod of recognition, the priest sat down beside Manickam. To his amusement, the rich moneylender quickly folded his cloth skirt closer around himself and edged away to a safe distance.

Manickam could control his emotions no longer. He blurted out angrily, "So! Instead of driving out the foreigner, you pick him up? You! You! A Brahman priest? You touch him and enter his house? You're an outcaste!"

He spat a long stream of *betel* juice to show his disgust. The red stream hit the dusty road and caused a dark spot on the ground. Ratnam thought idly that it reminded him of blood. He said nothing, and the moneylender continued, "You must be mad! Or else . . ." he smirked, "or else, you have a reason? I hear the white man is rich."

Ratnam tried to control his anger, and sat silent. Dassan squirmed, his shifty eyes darting uneasily between the two men. Ratnam finally broke the silence. "Remember, Manickam," he said, "we are under British rule. If the white man dies, you will be charged with murder. You know that!" He paused, then continued, "I've probably saved your life. I think the foreigner will live."

After another pause, the priest said, "I surely have broken caste. Do about that what you will. As for me, I'm not going through ceremonies, pilgrimages, and expense to gain restoration!" His courage mounted.

"Caste! What good is caste," he asked, lowering his voice, "when it leads you to murder? I'm tired, and both of you make me sick."

With that, Ratnam arose, motioned them to leave, and disappeared into his house. Once inside, he bolted the door and sank onto a mat. A feeling of extreme weariness and loneliness overcame him. Then he looked up to find Padmini hovering in the doorway. "Come," she said, "I have a cup of hot milk ready for you before you go to bed."

Chapter Eight
Ratnam Decides

"You took care of Manickam quickly, didn't you?" remarked Padmini with a smile as she handed Ratnam the cup of hot milk.

"Manickam likely thought he had me on his string," her husband said with a chuckle. "Come to think of it, he probably wanted to loan me money so that I could bribe my way back into the system. Well. . . ." The tall man shrugged his shoulders, then added, "he needn't bother. I'm not the priest in this village anymore."

"What do you mean, Ratnam?" his wife cried in alarm.

"Come, let's sit together, and I'll tell you about Manickam and Dassan. Then you'll see what I mean." When Ratnam recounted Manickam's edging away from him on the verandah, both husband and wife laughed aloud. "Come to think of it," said Padmini, "we do have silly customs."

24

Ratnam added more seriously, "But this upsets my well-ordered world. I'm an outcaste! Padmini, do you realize what that means?"

If the woman felt any heaviness or fear, she didn't show it. "We'll face this together," she said simply. He continued, "I don't feel I can advise others on religious matters when I'm in turmoil inside. I've been thinking about what Peter told me. Several days at home would give me a chance to sort things out."

"Do you have any plan?" she asked. "I'll do whatever I can to help."

He thought a little, then answered, "Yes, I'm going to pretend I'm ill. Keep people away—not that they will flock to enter!" He grimaced slightly, then chuckled. The situation hit him as ludicrous. "I'm an outcaste now, you know. Still . . ." and he turned to take her hand, "people will be people! Their curiosity will bring them here, so say anything. Tell them I have a contagious disease, if you want to!" They laughed together, sensing a bond as partners in a new adventure.

Padmini agreed, then busied herself with tidying the house and getting little Raju ready for bed.

"We must be quiet," she whispered as she tucked him in. "*Appa* is very, very tired."

"Is he sick?" asked the lad.

"Oh, maybe," Padmini answered absent-mindedly, and went to her husband.

In the morning some of Ratnam's friends came to see him. Before Padmini could meet them, Raju ran out and in a loud whisper informed them they must be quiet.

"*Appa* is very, very tired, and maybe he is sick," he said.

The men looked at Padmini who had just appeared. She merely nodded, adding, "He needs rest." They took the hint and left.

News of Ratnam's illness travelled fast throughout the village and expanded with each telling. Gossip declared him to be in serious condition. Worshippers cared for the cobra with more than usual attention. He must be very angry because the priest had entered the white man's house! Children soon observed their parents' treatment of the priest. They cursed Raju and avoided the white man's school. Mary heard the story and passed it on to

Peter. He felt greatly burdened for Ratnam, knowing his own responsibility for the incident. All Peter could do was trust the Lord to work out everything to His glory, and to that end, he prayed.

"But how can we be sure it's the truth?" questioned Mary.

"By going to see him," countered her husband.

"Good enough! Let's go tonight."

When the village settled to rest, with all lights out, the English couple walked quickly to Ratnam's house at the far end, near the temple. They didn't know what to expect, but were relieved when Padmini met them at the door and invited them in.

"I'm glad to meet you," she said shyly. "I've seen you only once from a distance, but my husband and son have told me so much, I feel I know you."

They entered at her request and sat on mats she offered.

Ratnam hastily tidied himself and came in to welcome his friends. Peter looked at him in amazement. "*Swamiji!*" he exclaimed. "You're looking fit! Do you know what people are saying about you?"

"What, Peter?" the tall man asked, smiling.

"They have you ready for the grave, by the act of the cobra!"

"How should the cobra know? I haven't been to the temple since I last saw you!" Ratnam chuckled, and Peter joined in appreciatively.

"How is it you aren't going?" the white man asked.

Ratnam's eyes twinkled. "If the reports reaching me are true, the cobra is getting far more attention than I ever gave him! I don't think he needs me now."

"What do you mean, *Swamiji?*" asked Mary. She sensed a spiritual yearning in this man.

"Seriously, *amma*," he responded, looking at Mary, "these days of quiet reflection have helped me decide to renounce caste and my position as a Brahman priest."

"Are you sure, *Swamiji?*" Inner joy flooded both Peter and Mary, and their faces glowed.

"I don't understand why," he concluded after telling of Manickam's visit and the resultant decision to not appear in public for awhile.

"I think I know the answer, *Swamiji*," Mary replied softly.

"You see, we've been praying much for you. We would like to see you accept the Lord Jesus Christ."

Padmini sat quietly to one side. She watched the guests constantly, and her mind whirled with questions. Peter opened the black book which he called the Holy Bible. From it he read such wonderful things that both Ratnam and his wife were visibly moved. Padmini looked around. Was the Living God in their house right now? Didn't they have to go to the temple to worship? Could God speak to them here—the very God who made the cobra?

Padmini, questing and yearning, glanced at her husband, and noted a look of peace on his face. He gave her a reassuring smile, and somehow, she was glad.

"I'd like to come to your home for more Bible reading tomorrow," Ratnam said. But Mary noted a wistful look on Padmini's face.

"Little sister, you can't leave the house, can you?" she asked. "May we come here instead? About the same time?" Padmini, much pleased, shyly nodded her assent.

"We must leave now," said Peter. "But first, if you don't mind, I'd like to pray. Is that all right?"

Ratnam didn't know what that meant, but he agreed. The English couple knelt down and Ratnam and Padmini did the same. They heard Peter speaking earnestly, as to a very close friend. Ratnam cautiously looked around to see if someone had entered. Padmini's eyes were shut. She thought somebody must have come, but feared to look.

Peter apparently felt this Jesus to be the answer to all of Ratnam's problems. Ratnam thought He must be extremely powerful and influential, too!

The prayer concluded, and they all stood up. Ratnam couldn't explain the sense of release which he felt. A great load had rolled away!

Ratnam and Padmini walked to the gate with their friends. He said quietly, "Please don't call me *Swamiji* anymore. I'm just Ratnam, and this is Padmini, my wife. And may we call you Peter and Mary?"

The white *amma's* eyes shone with joy. "Of course!" she exclaimed. "You're our new brother and sister in the Lord, aren't you? Now we're family!"

But soon, persecution struck. The next day, Ratnam's house was stoned.

Chapter Nine
A Friend in Need

Appu, a local shopkeeper in town, had been a close friend of Ratnam's through the years. He heard the gossip and determined to ferret out the truth. During the heat of the day, when everyone normally stayed indoors, Appu left the shop in the clerk's care and walked over to the priest's home. Padmini opened the door a crack in response to his call.

"I hear Ratnam is sick," Appu said. "Contagious disease, or what? I don't care. . . . I'm coming in!"

She gave him a shy smile as he added, "What's a friend for? You should have sent for me." Padmini pushed the door open, and he entered.

Hearing his voice, Ratnam walked out of his bedroom. Appu gave him a quick look and blurted out, "What's this nonsense about you being seriously ill? I've never seen you looking better! Out with it, man! What's the story?"

Ratnam laughed, then hugged his friend. With a twinkle in his eyes he remarked, "Since you enter the house of this untouchable, Appu, I presume you don't mind my embracing you? You're a true brother!"

With a smile Padmini murmured that she would make coffee and snacks, and hurried to the kitchen. Clearly, Appu was an ally in this battle.

After the initial banter, however, Ratnam fell silent. Appu waited, and finally his friend said, "You won't understand me. In fact, you may despise me; probably you will—even though we have been brothers."

"Out with it, man!" Appu's rotund frame shook as he shifted to a more comfortable position in his chair.

"But you may become my enemy, as have some of the others," Ratnam said with a sigh.

"I can take it, but I want the truth, Ratnam. We've been brothers for thirty years, and I don't see anything separating us now. Why should you even express doubt?"

The tall man looked at his companion intently. "Of course you've heard the story. . . ."

"I want your version of it, Ratnam," Appu remarked grimly. "I reserve the right to my opinion, but it's only proper that you speak."

"Why did I ever doubt you?" Ratnam responded with a sigh of relief. He recounted the whole matter, including Peter and Mary's visit the night before. Appu, thoroughly absorbed, followed the story closely, sometimes chuckling, then grunting an assent. When Ratnam finished, Appu grasped his hand and said, "You are a brave man, brother, and you did right. It's my turn to talk now. I wish I had as good a story as you."

He cleared his throat and began slowly, searching for words. "I've been a coward," he acknowledged, looking down. "From my store I've often listened to the white man preaching. Curiosity held me at first, but later on, his message gripped me. Frankly, I like him!"

Appu stood up and began to walk, as though to relieve his feelings. He turned toward Ratnam and said, "He's different from other English people I've seen, and deep within me, I respect his message. I'd like to learn more about this Lord Jesus, but I've been afraid to let anyone know of my interest." The man sat down again with a laugh, saying, "There! I've told you! We're in this thing together!"

"Appu!" Ratnam's eyes shone with joy. Jumping up, he pulled off his shirt, disclosing the sacred cord which he had never removed since the day he received it as a boy entering the adult world. "This is the moment!" he exulted. "I wondered when I should do this!" He pulled the cord over his head and cast it to the ground. "There! That's finished!" he said before his companion could interfere.

"You've renounced your heritage and your authority as a Brahman priest?" Appu whispered aghast.

Ratnam's face glowed. "For my Lord Jesus, Appu! I give myself to Him, and from this moment, I am His."

Too moved to speak, Appu could but grasp his hand. "I wish I had your courage," he murmured. Then he asked, "You're meeting the white man and his wife again? When?"

"Tonight, here in my home—late," answered his friend.

"You can count on me, too!" With a warm embrace, Appu left.

———

Later in the day Raju developed a high fever. "*Appa, Amma*," he called as he tossed from side to side. His mother knelt beside the mat and wondered what to do. Normally she would have taken special offerings to appease the cobra, but today she knew she would never step inside that temple again. To whom should she go now?

Raju looked up and whispered, "*Amma*! Won't you pray for me? The white *amma* says Jesus heals sick people."

Through Padmini's mind flashed the story she had heard Peter read from his black book. The Lord Jesus healed a blind man. But that was years ago! But she remembered the white *appa's* words: "He's not dead! He rose from the grave, and He's living! He heals today . . . just ask Him."

32

The woman also remembered her answer to the white *amma* when she asked, "Little sister, do you also believe in Jesus?" To which she replied, "I will, if I can test Him for myself and find Him true." Well, here was her chance.

"How do I pray, Raju?" she asked the child.

"Like you talk to me, *Amma*," he replied simply. "He's right here. The white *amma* says we can come to Him any time." Raju folded his hands together and closed his eyes. Padmini followed suit, and said, "God, Raju says you're right here. I wish I knew you! I'd like to know more. The white people say your name is Jesus. Lord Jesus, here I am, with my son, Raju. He's sick. Please make him well again. If you'll heal him, I'll always believe you and trust you." She didn't know what else to say, so Padmini rose quietly and went to work in the kitchen.

A short time later she suddenly felt a hand on her shoulder. She turned. Raju stood beside her, a big smile on his face.

"*Amma*," he said, "I'm hungry. See, *Amma*? Jesus healed me!" She threw her arms around him and found him cool and normal. "Son! Oh, son!" she exclaimed. "Of course I'll get you something to eat. What do you want?"

As she began to prepare the food, she whispered, "Jesus! I believe in you."

Half an hour later Ratnam entered to find his son eating a hearty meal of curry and rice. "What's this?" he asked as he patted the boy on the head. "I thought you were sick. Was that just make-believe?"

The boy shook his head vigorously. He looked up and said, "No, *Appa*! Jesus healed me. Ask *Amma*. She knows."

Ratnam glanced at his wife, and she looked down. Shyly, she told him of her prayer, and the Lord's immediate answer. "I believe, Ratnam," she confessed. He made no comment, but he was obviously pleased.

The tall man sat alone on the verandah for a long time, thinking things over. He sensed the beginning of a whole new life, something he had never before known.

Chapter Ten
Appu Faces a Decision

Confused by all that Ratnam had recounted, Appu felt he couldn't face his duties at the shop. He must take time to think! To everyone's surprise, he released his helpers early and closed the door. Then he turned toward the jungle trails.

Appu had never been a devout Hindu, but he continued the outward rites of religion to please the godly and upright priest. Diligence and hard work were his gods, if he had any. As a result, Appu held the high esteem of the community and his business prospered.

Could he afford to lose respect by favoring the foreigners and considering their message seriously? What about Rukmoni, his wife? She loved the luxurious life which her husband gladly gave her. Indeed, Appu delighted in his family. What would happen to his son, Prem Kumar, and his daughter, Premila, should he become a Christian? He wandered aimlessly through the woods, thinking seriously for several hours.

When Appu reached home, Rukmoni rushed to the door to greet him. "Uncle has come!" she exclaimed. "He's resting now. He told me my sister is engaged, and the marriage will be held next month." She chattered on, not noticing her husband's weariness. "Mother wants me to come soon and help her with the arrangements. Isn't that exciting?"

Rukmoni's eyes flashed as she talked. She was young and pretty, but oh, so full of herself, thought Appu. He sincerely loved her and desired her happiness. She continued, "Oh, Appu, I must have a new *sari* for the wedding . . . and these gold bangles are completely out of fashion! Could you have them melted and made into a new pattern?" she asked wistfully.

Seldom did Rukmoni consider others. In her excitement she

failed to note the strained expression on her husband's face. Must he choose between Jesus Christ and this beautiful woman? He pushed the thought aside. For the moment, he could cater to Rukmoni's whims, so he responded cheerfully, "That's good news about the wedding, my love. I'll see that you get everything you need. Take your bangles to the goldsmith and choose your pattern. But no more than one hundred *rupees*, mind you," he said with mock severity.

"A hundred *rupees*!" gasped his wife. "I can have these remade and buy an extra pair for that amount!"

Her eyes followed Appu as he went to the well to wash. She thought, my gods are really favoring me today! What if I had a husband like Lakshmi's. He beats her regularly. But then, she's a scatterbrain!

When Appu came, Rukmoni set a snack and hot coffee before him and dutifully served, chatting happily. She looked up as her uncle walked in. He slapped Appu on the back, making the man wince. Then he sat down to enjoy the meal and to give Appu all the news he had already heard from Rukmoni. Appu entered into the conversation, giving correct comments and asking the right questions, but his mind revolted. He wished this man were miles away.

Appu, the astute businessman, knew the routine, and watched it unfold. Uncle began the process by recounting his problems. Business was poor, he said, and he needed money to tide him over. After presenting his case, Appu suspected he'd try wheedling a loan which he never intended to return.

Rukmoni's husband thought quickly. Why not cut the ordeal short by anticipating his guest's request? The shopkeeper pulled five ten-*rupee* notes from his wallet and handed them to Rukmoni's uncle.

"Here, take this," he said magnanimously. "With that big wedding on your hands, I'm sure you will need some extra cash. This will help. No, that's all right. Don't feel obliged to repay! I'm glad to do this for the family."

Uncle gave Appu a quick glance. The shopkeeper continued, "I'm sorry I can't spend more time with you. I've got an important appointment this evening and must go now."

He turned to leave, then as an afterthought, said to Rukmoni, "Here, my love, take this for your new *sari*, and get some clothes for the children." With this, he handed her a hundred-*rupee* note. Before she could answer, he had gone.

Rukmoni and her uncle looked at each other in amazement. "What has happened to your husband?" he asked. Not expecting an answer, he said, "Well, I know when I'm not welcome! I'd better go on my way. Come as soon as you can." With that he rolled up his bundle, said goodbye to his niece, and left the house.

Appu took the path toward the woods. The cool, fresh evening air soon revived his drooping spirits, but not for long. As he rounded a bend, he saw a group of town elders sitting on Manickam's verandah. Too late Appu wished he had taken the other route; they already had spotted him.

Puturaj called out, "Here comes Ratnam's closest friend. We need you, Appu. Come, tell us what you think."

"Think about what?" the man asked as he sat on the mat pushed out for him. He respected Puturaj, not only for his age, but for being helpful when the white man was assaulted.

Appu didn't remain ignorant long. Manickam talked loudly, making all kinds of evil accusations against Ratnam. Dassan, his aide, gave quick assent to all his master said. Several others remained silent, but Puturaj argued in favor of Ratnam, contending that it was the duty of the priest to aid the foreigner in such a critical situation. Siromani agreed.

Puturaj said firmly, "If the white man had died, all of us would have been in serious trouble. Probably the murderer would have been hanged. Maybe that would have been a good thing."

Dassan jumped to his feet in a rage, but Manickam pulled him down. Angry words passed between Puturaj and Dassan, but when Dassan saw he had no support from the moneylender, the crisis passed.

Somebody mentioned that many villagers had already forgotten the incident. The foreigner had bought supplies at Appu's store today, then visited friends. Indeed, almost all the children had returned to the white *amma's* school. This was in the English couple's favor.

"Have you noticed how the white *amma* is gaining the confidence of our women?" asked one of the elders. "Look at Ramu's wife and children. None of us could help them because of Ramu."

Several murmured assent, and he continued, "All of you know he was a drunken wretch and his starving family went about in rags. But have you seen him lately?" The man looked around at his companions, then added, "No? Well, let me tell you. Ramu's working for the white man, gardening! He's given up drinking, believe it or not. . . . When I met him with his family in the bazaar yesterday, I scarcely recognized them! They were neat and clean! I tell you, something has happened to Ramu."

Manickam broke in, "Huh! Why are you impressed? Can't you see the white *amma* is buying their souls with money?"

Appu shouted, "Manickam! You temple-robber! All you think of is evil. You blackmail Ratnam. You tried to kill the white man. Dassan, you're no better! Have you ever earned an honest *rupee* in your life? All you do is trail after Manickam, and flatter him! You. . . ." Puturaj and Siromani jumped up and pulled Appu away, cutting short his tirade.

"That's enough, Appu," commanded Puturaj. "Let's get out of here." Under his breath he continued, "Come over to my house. I want to talk to you some more."

Everyone felt relieved that the men hadn't come to blows, and the group quickly disbanded, with Appu joining Puturaj and Siromani.

Not until they reached his house did Puturaj speak. "I'm concerned about Ratnam," he said slowly. "I've heard all sorts of rumors. I know he hasn't been to the temple since that incident in the bazaar. If he's sick, we should help him. Shouldn't we, Siromani?"

The younger man nodded, adding, "My wife went to the house, but Raju said his father wasn't seeing any visitors. Something is wrong!"

Puturaj nodded thoughtfully, then commented, "Ratnam never acted like this before. I know some are considering him an outcaste, but the fact is he did what all of us should have done! Instead of scorning him, we ought to thank him for saving the white man's life! What sort of thinking is this which turns good into evil?"

Appu listened quietly, not trusting himself to keep Ratnam's secret. Puturaj turned to him and laid his hand on Appu's arm. "You're his closest friend. Please go and find out for us. And here . . . give this to him," he said, shoving a tightly-rolled *rupee* note into Appu's hand. "I want him to accept this. Normally I would give it on the temple platter. I want Ratnam to know I care."

"Me, too," seconded Siromani, adding another note.

Appu tucked the money into the folds at the waist of his cloth skirt, and said, "I'll do what I can to bring you news tomorrow morning. You can meet me at the shop."

On returning home, Appu noted the uncle's absence. "He's gone?" he asked Rukmoni casually.

"Yes," she said, somewhat perplexed. "He usually stays several days."

"I have books to do tonight, Rukmoni, so I'll appreciate being alone right now." He began to check his daily accounts while his wife excused herself and prepared to retire. As soon as his family was sleeping soundly, Appu picked up his walking stick and slipped out. Except for a barking dog on the other side of the village, the street seemed deserted, with every light extinguished. Appu breathed deeply of the night air, and excitement made him quicken his steps.

Within his heart he knew he had decided. Though apprehension gripped him, the man's faith also leaped forward. He must follow Christ, regardless of personal cost! No more maneuvers of religiosity to Hindu deities. Appu, the thorough businessman, knew that commitment would cost. Persecution—like the stoning of Ratnam's house one recent night—could be expected. But Ratnam and he could stand together. It had always been so; it would continue.

Appu hastened his steps toward his friend's house.

Chapter Eleven
Appu Takes a Stand

Ratnam met Appu at the door, and they embraced warmly. Peter and Mary hadn't yet arrived. Just as well, thought Appu. He had much to share concerning the elders' meeting.

"The village is divided," he said. "Manickam and his gang are very angry, but Puturaj and Siromani stood up for you. In fact, they are much concerned about your welfare. Here, take this, Ratnam." Appu took the *rupee* notes from his bag and handed them to his friend. "They couldn't give this to you at the temple," he added, "so they sent it with me. They asked me to find out how you are."

Ratnam looked at his friend searchingly. How much had he disclosed?

Appu seemed to read his thoughts. He laughed, "No, Ratnam, I didn't tell them I'd been here!"

"Was there an elders' meeting?" his companion inquired.

"Was there ever!" exclaimed Appu with a short laugh. "You should have seen me, Ratnam, making a fool of myself."

"You? Appu, did you get angry?"

"Did I ever! I couldn't take Manickam's insults and accusations any longer. . . . I just happened into the meeting, too, on the moneylender's verandah, Ratnam. And then. . . ."

"Yes?"

Appu grinned sheepishly. "Well, I lost my temper," he said. "It's a good thing Puturaj and Siromani were there to make me shut up." He chuckled, then added, "If I had my way, I'd have beaten them up! It's good you weren't there."

Ratnam touched his friend's shoulder and said simply, "Thank you, Appu. I know I can depend on you, but please take care of yourself. We don't need any more casualties around here."

40

Ratnam felt deeply about these men who trusted him as their friend and priest. What would Puturaj and Siromani do when they learned the truth? He felt a sudden pull of the old life, but quickly rejected it. The tall man slowly rolled the money into the folds at the waist of his *lungi*, then went to the door to answer the knock he heard.

"Come in," he said, bowing to Peter and Mary. They looked surprised at the shopkeeper's presence, but Ratnam commented, "He's my best friend. We have been brothers for years, and when others forsake me, Appu stands true. He is here because both he and I desire to know more about God." Looking for support from Appu, he asked, "Isn't that right?"

Padmini entered the room, and interestingly enough, it was she who broke into the conversation at this point. "I want to know more about your God," she said with a smile. "I'm finished with the cobra god, and with offerings and *puja* at the temple! I know your God is true because I proved Him. He made Raju well!"

She paused, uncertain, but with a little encouragement from Mary, told the entire story, adding, "Now I believe."

Ratnam, surprised at her openness, nevertheless felt proud of his wife. How had she overcome her natural shyness? As for Appu, Rukmoni flashed before his mind, and he wondered how soon he would hear her also declare her faith in Jesus.

Mary was speaking. "Yes, Padmini, God is like a father. He delights to answer the prayers of His children. Did you thank Him?"

"Oh, no, I didn't think of that," Raju's mother replied. "How ungrateful I am. Maybe God won't hear me again." She seemed distressed at the thought, but Mary laughed and took her hand. "That's all right, Padmini," she said kindly. "God isn't like that. I had to learn to say thanks, too, you know. Now, let's ask Peter to say thanks for all of us. We're so glad that Raju is well again."

She bowed her head, and the others followed. Peter began to speak so intimately and directly that Appu, startled, glanced around. His eyes met Ratnam's; his friend's smile reassured him.

"Who were you talking to?" asked Appu when Peter finished.

"To God, our heavenly Father," the white man replied.

"Now let me tell you more about Him." He opened the Holy Bible and explained the wonderful news of salvation. Appu heard the whole story for the first time. This is strange—and wonderful! he thought.

"Where is Jesus?" he asked. "Can we meet Him?"

"Yes," said Peter. "The Lord Jesus is alive. You know how you ask the spirit of a deity to come into an idol? That's something that men make with their own hands, Appu."

The man nodded, then thought of the cobra. "What about the cobra?" he asked. "That's a living thing, not an idol."

"But it also has been created," responded Peter. "And the God who made the cobra made you and me, too. You see, Appu, we don't need to bow down to things God created. Rather, the Creator Himself desires our worship."

"But where is He? How can I know Him?" the man asked, although he remembered hearing messages from Peter which answered this question.

"He came to us, Appu, in Jesus Christ, His son. Through Jesus, we come to the Father. And through Jesus, we receive the Spirit of God in our lives. Where does Jesus live?" Peter looked at Mary and smiled, saying, "In her, and in me! How do we know? Because He puts His love in us, and we act like Him."

"Oh!" Appu's eyes were shining. Strange and wonderful it might be, but now he could understand why Peter never short-changed him when paying his bills. He could see love shining out through those blue eyes. It was Jesus, thought Appu.

"Now it's very late, and we must go," said Peter. "But before we leave, is there anything you would like us to pray about?"

Appu ventured, "The elders are meeting me at the shop tomorrow, and I must report on Ratnam. What shall I say?" he asked earnestly.

Ratnam spoke up. "Tell them, Appu, I'm no longer their priest. I've decided to become a Christian. From now on, I won't go to the temple. The cobra god cannot help us. I will follow. . . ."

"Not so fast, Ratnam," interrupted Appu. "Are you sure? Have you considered?"

Padmini joined in quickly, "My husband is right, Appu. We've decided, and we can't go back now. We'll trust the Lord

Jesus for ourselves and for Raju, too." She turned to the shop-keeper and said softly, "And Appu, if I'm right, you've decided also. Haven't you?"

Her directness startled Appu, but he responded positively. "Yes, Padmini, I've decided. But I have much to do first. I can't come right away." He added thoughtfully, "My wife isn't ready. She's not prepared for what I have to tell her. But I will come; just give me a little more time."

Peter's prayer praised God for the commitment of these three to Jesus Christ, and he asked guidance for Appu in speaking to the elders. Before leaving, Peter warned, "You will have to face opposition, perhaps persecution. But don't be afraid. Jesus has promised us His continual presence. He won't fail you!"

They were all filled with joy, and after a few words of admonition and reassurance, they parted.

Ratnam and Padmini talked until almost daybreak. Shortly after dawn Ratnam started for District Headquarters on business. On the way back, he stopped at a barber shop and had a haircut. His long hair, symbol of his status as priest in the temple, belonged to the old life. The sacred cord was abandoned when he changed internally; now an outward change must come so that all would know. With a new determination and look of peace and joy, Ratnam turned homeward to face the stares of his people.

Appu would long remember that evening! As he left Ratnam, their hands clasped as though sealing a pact and their eyes met for a moment. Then Appu disappeared into the darkness. He breathed deeply of the fragrant night air. Within, he sensed profound peace. He had heard Peter pray. Now Appu bowed his head and spoke earnestly to the Lord Jesus Christ about the step he had taken and the difficult path ahead.

Next morning he felt that life had just begun—or was *he* different? His bath and morning exercises over, Appu played with the children until Rukmoni served his breakfast. As he sat down he asked, "Are you going to have your bangles remade today? And you'll buy your new *sari?*" Rukmoni, surprised at his interest, smiled and replied, "Yes, I'm going shopping. I'll show you when you return this evening."

Just then the manager came for the keys.

"Sundar! You look troubled. What's the matter?" Appu asked.

"My wife's ill again, master," the young man replied. "We can't seem to find the cause."

"I think we can do something for her," Appu replied kindly. "Go, open the shop. I'll come soon."

A few minutes later he walked the short distance to the general store, set advantageously in the center of the marketplace. "God has been good to me," he thought as he read his name, R. P. Appu, in small lettering on the sign. Walking into the shop, Appu took his place on a well-padded platform about the size of a double bed. Oblong cushions supported his rotund frame. To his side he placed a steel cash box and his bright orange turban. Nearby, a small brass box contained *betel* leaves. These were wrapped in a red-stained, moist cloth with other ingredients to make *pan.*

He surveyed the shop with satisfaction. His business was prospering. Groceries and bags of grain filled the front areas; at the back, kitchen supplies, hardware, and clothing stocked the shelves. As a convenience to the community, with its advantageous location, the general store served as a meeting place for friends.

Customers arrived as soon as Sundar opened the doors. When the sun rose higher in the heavens, and business slackened,

Appu called his manager and told him, "The white *amma* lives near the pond. Take your wife to her. She knows about women's ailments. I'm sure she can help."

The young man looked surprised. He spoke haltingly, "But, sir . . . she's . . . a . . . foreigner! How can I?"

"That's all right, Sundar. You don't need to fear," continued Appu. "She won't ask you into the house. Just take your wife and listen to what the white *amma* tells her. Here are three *rupees* for any medicine you may need. You can go early today. I'll stay and care for everything."

Sundar, speechless, gratefully accepted the money and returned to his work, but Appu called after him, "Young man, I hear you've been visiting the witch doctor. Don't go to him anymore. It's useless, and he's not a good man."

Sundar wondered, what's happened to him? He's unusually kind and thoughtful today. I think he really cares!

Both Appu and his manager felt a new lift, with the day looking brighter.

Mid-morning, Arputham came bounding into the shop. He had become a handyman for the missionaries. As usual, he brought a long list of groceries to be purchased for his "home," as he called it. The boy collected the supplies and placed them in his bag. Appu got up and added a pound of brown sugar. "Here, take this to *amma*," he said. "This is a gift from the shop." A broad grin spread across Arputham's face. He thanked Appu, paid his bill, and jumped on his cycle. The tinkling of the cycle bell echoed what Appu felt in his inner being. This was a good day!

Chapter Twelve
Appu Reports on Ratnam

The sun rode high in the heavens when the group of village elders gathered outside the general store.

"Come along, gentlemen," called Appu cheerily. "Let's sit under the shade of the old pipal tree. It's cooler there."

Puturaj and Siromani led the way. Appu noted idly that Manickam, the moneylender, and Dassan, his henchman, were conspicuously absent. When each had seated himself and the hum of friendly conversation had died down, Appu cleared his throat loudly to gain attention. Then he went right to the point.

"Gentlemen," he began, "Puturaj and Siromani asked me to visit Ratnam to determine the trouble, as you know. I went last night, and found the family looking both fit and well."

He paused and glanced their direction. "Ratnam wants me to thank you for your generous gifts. In fact, he was deeply touched by your thoughtfulness." The men nodded their heads in acknowledgement.

Appu continued, "He has a warm regard for all of you, and he asks me to convey his good wishes." A murmur of approval rippled through the group.

Now the shopkeeper seemed to grope for words. "Ratnam says . . . he's asked me to tell you . . . no, he doesn't hold ill will toward anyone. But he says he can no longer be your priest."

The men looked at each other in disbelief. Before anyone could speak, Appu continued, "He . . . well . . . in fact . . . he said he'll be glad for anyone to visit him. Though now he is . . . well, he says he's an untouchable! He broke caste, as you know, when he entered the white man's house."

The men gasped in amazement, too stunned to speak. They shifted uneasily. Puturaj found his voice first.

"You mean . . . he's not trying to retain his rights as our Brahman priest? You mean he's taking this untouchable business seriously?"

"Well," said Appu with a chuckle, "we have our friends Manickam and Dassan to thank for that. Ratnam tells me they came to see him, and the moneylender pulled his skirts about him so that he wouldn't get defiled!"

That broke the tension, and the men laughed. They could visualize the episode very clearly. Who among them didn't know Manickam?

"Let's get this straight, Appu," said Siromani seriously. "You mean Ratnam's not going to try for reinstatement? He's not going to take up his temple duties again?"

Appu nodded, then replied, "That's what he told me."

"Then what?" Puturaj whispered, as though unable to voice his worst fears.

Appu lifted his hands in a hopeless gesture. Inwardly he prayed, "Lord Jesus, I need you. Are you there?" Then he answered earnestly, "All of us know Ratnam. He is godly and true." Every head nodded.

"He saw divine love in the Englishman," continued Appu. "When the white man refused to become bitter against his enemies, Ratnam realized God was in their lives, moving them to love instead of hate. We know many in our village are treating the white man badly—despite the fact that he's good. And the white *amma* is teaching our children and giving our wives medicine."

Several of the elders nodded. Puturaj spoke up, "It's a shame we can't treat guests in a better manner. Yes, they're good people! Not at all like the government officials we've seen. But does that mean we should follow their religion?"

"Oh!" said everybody. Appu continued, "I suppose each one of us has our private opinion on that, Puturaj. I'm merely reporting on Ratnam's feeling about it." The men settled to hear, and the shopkeeper said, "He's been spending his days and nights in meditation and prayer. He's seen something of the white people, inquiring where this divine love comes from. And now he's decided to follow Jesus Christ, as the Author of this new kind of life."

"Oh!" whispered Puturaj, while the others maintained shocked silence.

"He's going to follow the white man's religion?" the wizened elder asked.

"Yes, my friends. Don't think for a moment you can change his mind. Our Ratnam is a godly man, and he's ready to do anything he thinks is right. He has proved that to us already."

The implications of Appu's report began to sift through each man's consciousness. No priest? He had forsaken them, turned from what he taught them to believe? Now they were leaderless. Who would—who could replace Ratnam? He was truly a great man, one whom they loved and respected as their religious head.

In the pregnant silence which prevailed, Appu rose and said, "Now, friends, you'll excuse me. But let me urge you to go and visit Ratnam for yourselves. He is still your friend."

Chapter Thirteen
The First Baptism

Since Dassan assaulted Peter, the village had been divided. Some favored letting the white people stay; others opposed them. Many appreciated the school and nursing care which the white *amma* gave their women and children, and they could speak no ill of her.

The men, generally speaking, accepted Peter. Despite his blonde hair and blue eyes, he identified in any way possible, even to wearing Indian garb in preference to his own. He accompanied friends to their fields or work and spent much time on a one-to-one basis.

Manickam and Dassan, however, had a following from among those who enjoyed heckling the foreigners. Despite the opposition, Peter and Mary walked among the villagers with serene countenance and happy smiles. It troubled their enemies to see them meet insults with kindness, taunts with gestures of friendship. Manickam and Dassan redoubled their efforts, now widening their targets to include all Christians.

Peter's friendship with Puttappa, the shoe cobbler, began when the white man took his sandals for mending. Considered an outcaste, Puttappa sat by the road under a tree near Peter's home. With his anvil and hammer, his pieces of leather and string, the man cut out and sewed strong shoes for the entire community.

Peter found him not only knowledgeable, but keen and alert to spiritual concepts. Since both the white man and the cobbler were considered outcastes by the community, nobody noticed Peter spending a great deal of time with him.

Then came the news that Puttappa and his family had declared faith in Jesus Christ and were going to be baptized publicly in the pond near the white man's home. Already preparations were underway. Christians from another village, half a day's journey away, had arrived and were staying with the missionaries. The white *amma* and *appa* seemed to belong to a big, happy family.

Manickam called Dassan and said, "Go! Burn the white man's house, and drive every Christian from the village."

Dassan laughed, his shifty glance darting here and there. "When?" he asked.

"Tomorrow," whispered the moneylender.

Then his face blanched as he watched a Britisher get off his horse in front of the general store.

"Who is it?" asked Manickam. "Who dares disturb our peace?"

"I'll find out, master," replied Dassan, and he hastily joined the crowd of bystanders.

"An Englishman lives here?" the British District Magistrate inquired of Appu.

"Yes, your honor," the shopkeeper replied with a smile and a bow. "Welcome to our village, sir. May I give you a cup of hot coffee before you meet Mr. Peter?"

"Thank you very much," the officer responded with alacrity. He followed Appu into the shop while Sundar dispatched a messenger to inform the white man of the Britisher's arrival. Peter left word with Mary to include the officer for lunch, and hurried to meet their guest.

"He's in there," said Puturaj, pointing to the general store. "Appu is giving him some hot coffee."

"How kind of Appu! Do you know who the gentleman is, Puturaj?"

The village elder rubbed the back of his bald head and answered, "The new District Magistrate, I believe, *appa*."

With the highest ranking government officer of the area in the village at that particular time, Dassan's courage failed, and the plan to burn the white man's house was shelved for the time being. Both Manickam and Dassan had reason to lie low in the presence of the law.

Moreover, in the long talk he had with Peter, the officer learned the mission needed land for a school and farm. Together, they settled on a piece on the outskirts of the village, yet near enough to identify with the community.

The next day Arputham brought a friend to the general store. Both filled large baskets with over ten *rupees'* worth of produce. "It's for our big family," said Arputham, then added, "I'm going to be baptized tomorrow in the pond. Please come, Appu. You've been so good to me." Turning to other customers, he said, "And that goes for the rest of you, too."

"And who is your friend?" asked the shopkeeper.

"He's Jason, and he lives in Hosur, sir. He was baptized six months ago."

Many of the customers turned to look at the two young teenagers, and sensing their opposition, Arputham and his friend quickly completed their purchases and hurried back to the shelter of the mission compound.

A hum of excited discussion covered the marketplace. Everybody knew Arputham! They had seen him as a cheeky, whining beggar—hanging around their stalls and stealing anything he could lay hands on. But look at him now! His quiet, friendly manner made him a favorite. What he was today bore no resemblance to that earlier existence! The change spoke for itself, nor could anyone deny it.

However, his spontaneous invitation to attend his baptism came as a surprise. True, he had been a beggar on the street. But he was still an Indian, one of them. What right did this boy have to espouse a foreign religion?

Amidst the controversy, Appu's outspoken support for the boy bore weight. He said firmly, "I'm going! Yes, I'm going, simply because Arputham asked me to come. I'd far rather see him as he now is instead of the thief who caused me so much trouble before." All within earshot also privately determined to attend the baptismal service, although none knew what to expect.

When the first strains of song wafted over the village early Sunday morning, small groups of twos or threes started toward the pond. Arputham looked handsome in his new clothes. Puttappa and his family waited quietly beside the white man. The onlookers quickly seated themselves apart from the Christians, but near enough to see and hear everything. Ratnam and Appu also came, sitting near the Christians. Even Manickam and Dassan wanted to see, but sat on the other side from everyone else.

Ratnam's first public appearance since the assault on Peter would have caused more stir had the crowd not been captivated by what was happening in the pond. Many of his former friends gave Ratnam a few inquisitive glances, promising themselves to speak to him afterwards.

The singing concluded. A visitor, holding a black book like the one the white *appa* carried, read and then spoke. Although everyone could hear, not many spectators understood. It all seemed strange! A hush settled over the group as the white *appa* waded into the water until it reached above his knees. This was the moment!

One by one the applicants, some having come from other villages, entered the water and were baptized by Peter. To those uninitiated in the ways of Christians, the words sounded like a *mantra*, some sort of incantation.

Arputham came last. He stepped out boldly, and faced his neighbors and friends. "I want you to know why I'm here today," he said clearly. "You've seen me as a beggar, haven't you?" Heads nodded in agreement. "But look at me now! I'm cleaned up— inside and out! You say the white people did this? Oh, I know God used them to tell me about a better way than the one I knew.

But I want you to know it is Jesus who cleaned me and forgave my sins—all the lying and stealing I used to do! You know! I'm different now, and it's Jesus who made me what I am. I love Him and I want to follow Him in baptism today." With a smile he turned and walked into the water while a hush settled over the entire crowd.

Some who carried stones with which to pelt the Christians quietly dropped them. They felt ashamed as they, too, saw a better way!

———

Ratnam and Appu watched that first baptism keenly. They continued Bible study with Peter and Mary, and one day announced their intention to be baptized. Padmini gladly supported her husband. Not so, Rukmoni! She shouted, "How can you disgrace your family like this? Do you realize you make us outcastes, despised by everyone? I'll lose all my friends! I'm going back home! In any case, I'm leaving tomorrow for the wedding, but I'm warning you, Appu, I'm not coming back! I won't live with you any longer!"

She burst into sobs, throwing herself on the mat. Appu, greatly distressed, tried to soothe her. "Rukmoni," he pleaded, "please think it over before you make any final decision. It's good you're going tomorrow for the wedding. It will give you a chance to consider."

He gently touched her gold bangle which he had given her at their marriage, and said, "If you ever need me, Rukmoni, and you can't come yourself, just send the bangle. I will know."

Hastily leaving the room so that his wife wouldn't notice his pent-up emotions, he instructed the servants to help her get ready to leave. After the oxcart was loaded, Rukmoni and the children started off early next morning. Appu gave the cartman a *rupee* and ordered him to take his family safely to their destination.

That Sunday Ratnam, Padmini, and Appu were baptized. This visible break with the old life shook the village. The very foundations of their Hindu society were threatened. To have their former priest and an influential man like Appu become Christians brought tremendous upheaval and demanded action.

The Christians' fate would have been much worse except for the property which they now owned. Ratnam became supervisor of the mission farm. Supervising the building work and planting of rice fields and vegetable gardens kept him busy. The farm also afforded work to those who stepped out of the Hindu society.

Because of his responsibilities, Ratnam soon moved from his former home near the temple to a smaller house on the mission land. Peter and Ratnam worked together on a plan to make the Christians self-supporting. Both felt strongly that new believers should retain their independence economically and not become mission wards.

With the exception of Appu, who continued in his own home, it became apparent that opposition wouldn't allow Christians of lesser means to continue living in the village. Ratnam and Peter began to think about housing for converts as part of their expansion program. A church, school, and medical center would strengthen the importance of the new community and bring non-Christians to their door.

Interestingly enough, despite the beatings and other insults, the new Christian community grew and continued to impact the village for good.

Chapter Fourteen

Rukmoni's World Collapses

The villagers long remembered the splendid wedding in the home of Rukmoni's parents. Appu's wife flitted gracefully among the guests, serving everyone. She wore a thick, maroon-colored silk *sari* with a heavy gold border. Her diamond nose-stud and matching earrings flashed fire, and her new bangles were the envy of many women. Her delicate anklets tinkled; a gold belt studded with colorful gems encircled her slender waist. She was lithe, and her figure retained its youthful charm. Yes, Rukmoni was lovely, but very conscious of her beauty!

The feasting and ceremonies lasted ten days. Only after that did the household settle into normal routines. Now Rukmoni's memory came alive. How was Appu? She remembered her burst of anger when he told her his decision to become a Christian. She had hid her secret, not wanting to spoil her sister's wedding. Now she felt concern. Had Appu really been baptized? What change would it make in him? How could she ever return to a Christian husband? Yet she knew he loved her. Apprehension and dread took over as Rukmoni looked into a bleak future.

News traveled slowly. True, some Christians lived in a nearby village, but they were considered outcastes, untouchables! Little did Rukmoni and her parents suspect that this strange religion would so soon affect their personal lives.

At first the rumor was vague—the temple priest and someone else had been baptized. Then Appu's name came into the story. Alarmed, Rukmoni's father sought information from every available source, only to have the rumor confirmed. He stomped his foot in anger and threatened dire consequences should Appu ever come on his property again. Rukmoni's mother wailed as though her son-in-law had died. Perhaps that would have been better, she said. He had broken caste and disgraced the family. Now her daughter would be considered a widow!

The proud, beautiful Rukmoni suddenly became the object of scorn and disgrace. Her parents openly berated her. In the marketplace her friends avoided contact, and she could sense their ridicule as they told each other, "Her husband has become a Christian!"

Worse than the scorn and taunts was the fact that her mother tried to turn the children against her. Her parents took Prem Kumar and Premila to the temple regularly. The priest shaved Prem Kumar's head, leaving a tuft of hair on the back. As for Rukmoni, she offered flowers and curds to the family deity, but found no solace. Appu's beautiful wife, Rukmoni, found her world in shambles.

Deeply depressed, one evening she fled the village, going to a small clump of trees some distance away. There she flung herself on the soft leaves, weeping loudly and bitterly and wishing she could die.

In her sorrow she didn't hear approaching footsteps. Suddenly a gentle voice spoke, and Rukmoni felt a hand on her shoulder. "No, no," the voice said, "you must not weep so! Please tell us about your trouble. Perhaps we can help you."

The stranger took her arm and tried to lift her. Rukmoni sat up, surprised and somewhat alarmed. She looked into the lovely face of an older woman who knelt beside her.

"I'm Kanama," said the woman. "And my friend here is Salome. We were passing when we heard you, and came to see if we could help."

Rukmoni dried her tears. Meanwhile Salome also sat down and opened her bag. She brought out some homemade vegetable patties and a flask of hot coffee. She carefully poured a glass full of the liquid, then offered it to the distressed girl. Rukmoni accepted it gratefully.

"Would you like to share your troubles with us, or would you rather return home right away?" asked Kanama.

"Oh, you are so kind," she murmured. Rukmoni had never experienced such tactful love and kindness before. These strangers inspired confidence and she found herself talking easily.

"My husband has disgraced me and our family," she ventured. "He has become a Christian," she continued almost in a whisper, hanging her head. Again she began to weep, crying, "It is as though he died! I am a widow!"

In her preoccupation, Rukmoni didn't notice the glance which passed between her two companions. They said nothing, but waited for her to continue. "Why did he do it?" Rukmoni burst out.

Finally Kanama spoke, "Tell us more, little sister, then perhaps we can help you."

The girl lifted her tear-stained face to the lovely smile of her new friend. It encouraged her to say, "I cursed him and ran away from home when he told me he wanted to be baptized. I threatened never to live with him again! He didn't try to stop me, just looked heartbroken and hugged Prem Kumar and Premila as though he couldn't let go."

"It sounds as though your husband loves both you and your family," observed Kanama.

"Oh, he does!" sobbed Rukmoni as memory overtook her.

After a pause, she wiped her eyes and continued, "He made all the arrangements for me to come here to my parents' home and gave me more money than I needed. Now my parents have found out, and they have turned against me. I might as well die!"

"No, no, don't weep," said Salome. "See, we're here to help you!"

Suddenly the incongruity of the situation pressed in upon Rukmoni. "*Ammas*," she exclaimed, "how is it that both of you have come here, right now? Just in time—and with coffee, too!"

Kanama put her arm around the girl. Drawing her close she said, "I think it's because you needed us, Rukmoni. Will you be angry with us, too? We're also Christians, for about a year. We know how you feel. We used to feel that way. I hated Christians until I learned to know the Lord Jesus Christ. Now Salome and I love Him, and we come here regularly to read and pray together. That's how we found you. You see, little sister, the Lord Jesus sent us. He knew you needed help!"

The girl shuddered, and drew back. Christians! Christians! Could she never get away from them? She covered her face in her hands to rid herself of those two beautiful ladies who looked at her so lovingly. And she needed love!

The women began to sing softly, a touching lyric about Jesus being the Good Shepherd, going out to find the lost lamb in the thicket. Rukmoni couldn't help but listen, and suddenly she felt she was that lamb. If Jesus cared that much for her, why should she resist?

She listened quietly, then said, "Oh, thank you for that beautiful song. I think I'm that lamb, and you've come to find me."

"Little sister," said Kanama, "the Lord Jesus sent us. We'd like to tell you more about him."

Suddenly Rukmoni began to laugh. "Do you realize I've eaten your food and drunk your coffee? And now I'm an outcaste, too? Like Appu?" Her face suddenly took on a peaceful look as she continued, "Please tell me about Jesus. If Appu loves Him, I want to love Him, too."

"Appu?"

"My husband, and a very dear friend of Ratnam who used to be our village priest. But both Ratnam and his wife Padmini have been baptized, as well as Appu, since I left. We received word only last week, although it happened about a month ago."

Kanama and Salome looked at each other again, and Salome observed, "We heard about the village priest, didn't we?"

Kanama nodded, and Rukmoni continued softly, "I suppose everybody knows about it now. Padmini came to me one day to tell me about Jesus. I spat in her face, and chased her out of my house." She dropped her head in deep distress.

Salome put her arm around Rukmoni and spoke softly, "You want to become a Christian, too, don't you?" she asked.

"Is it possible? Can I?" cried the girl eagerly.

"Yes, it's possible. We'll help you," said Kanama. "Let me tell you what it means to believe in Jesus."

No preacher ever had a more attentive audience than Kanama did. Rukmoni soaked in every word, asking questions when she didn't understand. After Kanama prayed, Appu's wife began to pray. Hesitatingly at first, then with confidence, she said, "God, I'm such a proud woman, and I've done so many wrong things. Please forgive me. I want to be a Christian like Padmini, like Appu and Ratnam."

She stopped, lost in thought. Finally she looked at her two companions with a smile. "It's all right," she said, "I'll go back to my husband, and we'll be Christians together."

"Would you like to meet us here again tomorrow?" asked Salome.

Rukmoni lifted a radiant face. "I'd love it," she said simply. "I'll come at the same time."

With a short prayer they parted.

The house was empty when Rukmoni arrived home, and she was glad. She had time to tidy her room and talk to Jesus as she had heard Kanama doing. A great desire welled up within her to return to Appu, and she prayed that God would soon bring this to pass.

Chapter Fifteen
The Gold Bangle

Rukmoni met her two friends at the appointed time the next day and they talked and prayed together. Much encouraged, she told them of her desire to return to her husband. But she faced a great hurdle—she must first tell her parents!

Kanama looked troubled. What would happen to Rukmoni?

"Perhaps they won't allow you to come here," she suggested. "Shall we meet you at your home?"

"No, no!" protested the girl. Her memory of insulting Padmini was fresh in her mind. Under no condition did she want her parents to treat these lovely women in a similar way. "No, please!" she reiterated.

"What can we do to help you?" inquired Salome.

"I'll try to meet you here, as usual," Rukmoni replied. "But if I don't come, then. . . ."

"Yes?" prodded Kanama gently.

"You must send a message to my husband. Tell him I want to return home, but I can't—because of my parents. Tell him to come and take me away."

"How can we convince him this is true, and not a trap?" asked Salome thoughtfully.

Rukmoni looked at her bangle. "Here, take this." she said, slipping it off her wrist and handing it to Salome. It was ornate, obviously of value. "It is the first one Appu gave me at our marriage. We've had an understanding it would always be a means of communication, a symbol of peace. He'll understand."

Rukmoni turned and hurried away before they could see her tears. Kanama and Salome watched her leave, then prayed earnestly for this girl whom both of them had come to love. "Take care of her, Lord. We sense she is facing more than she can handle alone!"

Rukmoni's newfound joy sustained her through that walk home. They had called her "sister," as though she belonged! They had said, "Even though you aren't yet baptized, Rukmoni, you belong to Jesus Christ, and that makes you our true sister. Baptism will follow."

Upon entering the house, she greeted her mother cheerily. This only irritated the older woman and she shouted, "Who have you been meeting on the sly? You come back with a smirk on your face! What insolence!"

Rukmoni stood shocked and speechless. How could her mother insinuate that her daughter had done evil, especially when Rukmoni's newfound experience in Jesus was so very real? Anger made her flush, but suddenly love and pity took its place. She turned to leave, when a heavy hand struck her and stunned her momentarily. She cowered, and through her tears recognized her father, arm upraised, ready to strike again.

"First you explain to me where you have been, and whom you have been seeing," he yelled. "Your husband disgraces us, and now you are meeting someone on the quiet. Who is it? Speak up, girl, or I'll break every bone in your body!"

"No, no, not that!" Rukmoni cried, terrified. "I only talked with two women. I was so distressed, I thought I would take my life, but they helped me. They're Christians. I want to return to my husband, with my children. Please let me go," she pleaded, and fell at her father's feet.

Shocked silence! Then her father yanked her to her feet and hit her again and again. "There—take that—and that—and that!" he shouted. She looked imploringly at her mother, but the woman spat red *betel* juice into Rukmoni's face.

Suddenly Rukmoni saw a third person, smiling upon her in pity and love. He wore a crown of thorns and blood trickled down His cheeks. He beckoned, and Rukmoni stretched out her arms. "Lord Jesus," she whispered, bowing her head.

Awed by something they didn't understand, her parents quickly moved away. The mother spoke first. "Don't you dare step out of this house without first telling me where you are going," she demanded. "And don't you dare speak to those women again. You stay here—and work! Ammu is leaving. You'll cook for the family!"

"And listen to me," shouted her father. "From now on, you'll eat and sleep with the servants. Do you hear? Don't you dare tell anyone what you told us!"

Rukmoni was so aware of the Lord's presence that the beating and shouting seemed insignificant. She turned slowly and went to her room, expecting to find painful bruises on her body. Yes, there were marks! Why didn't she feel pain? Then part of a verse Kanama had shown her in the Bible came back, "He was wounded . . . bruised . . . by His stripes we are healed." Rukmoni laughed with sheer joy!

After a refreshing bath, the girl dressed in a plain cotton *sari* and reported to the kitchen. Her life of luxury had gone!

Ammu, the faithful family servant, had lived in her parents' home longer than Rukmoni could remember. Now she was leaving to live with her grandson in another village. As Rukmoni entered, the old woman threw her arms around her and held her tightly.

"Never did I think I would see such things in my home!" she sobbed. "I wish I wasn't going blind. I'd stay and take care of you, my child."

"Don't worry, Ammu," the girl said, patting her gently. "I'll be all right. You taught me to cook, so I'll do my best to give my parents good food. The trouble will blow over, and I'll return to my husband. Some day," and she patted Ammu lovingly, "someday I'll visit you in your new home in the village."

Ammu smiled, and the two women walked out into the garden, hand in hand.

The days passed quickly, without incident. Rukmoni longed to see her new friends again, to share her experiences with them. But in her loneliness, the face of the Lord Jesus continued to bring her daily comfort. Her parents, afraid to touch her again, constantly scolded her instead, and tried to embitter her children against her.

The servants initially took advantage of Rukmoni, but her capabilities and kindness quickly won their respect. In fact, her presence in the kitchen kept everything running smoothly.

Kanama and Salome visited the grove of trees several times, hoping to meet Rukmoni again. When she didn't come, they concluded that her parents had stopped her from coming. They

shared the story with their pastor, Gnanakan, and the small congregation. Immediately, Rukmoni's plight became a major concern.

The group decided to send Pastor Gnanakan and a brother to personally deliver her message to her husband.

"Here, Pastor, take the bangle," said Kanama, handing it over. "Rukmoni's husband will understand what it means."

By the next evening the men reached Appu's village. They found a warm welcome at Peter's house and a good meal did much to revive them. Ratnam was there, checking over some plans with Peter. The missionary viewed him thoughtfully.

"Ratnam," he said, "our guests need to see Appu right away. But for his sake, . . ." he looked at the former priest speculatively, "don't you think it better if not so many of us go?"

Ratnam nodded, and Peter continued, "You take Pastor Gnanakan. Brother Marcus can stay here with Mary and me. And we'll keep them overnight."

As he and the pastor walked down the road, Ratnam said, "What a blessing that it's this late. You likely realize we're suspect, as Christians. Even Appu! But because of his position and wealth, he's allowed to stay in his own home, and people come to his shop." The former priest laughed. "Funny, isn't it? The opposition will beat one person, but spare another—if he helps meet their needs!"

They walked in silence the rest of the way to the large house near the general store. Appu had been reading his Bible and praying for the return of his family. The house seemed lonely without them! He had just started reading another book when a knock interrupted his thoughts.

"Ratnam!" he said, recognizing the code which the two friends had used for years. He rose swiftly, and opened the door. "Come in, come in!" Ratnam and Appu embraced warmly, then Ratnam turned to his companion. "Appu," he said, "meet Pastor Gnanakan from a village near Rukmoni's home. He brings news of her."

"Oh!" exclaimed Appu, then decided to be cautious. He turned to his guest and greeted him warmly. "Did you meet my wife?" he questioned after the men took their seats.

"No, I haven't seen her," the man replied. "But two ladies from my congregation have been in touch with her."

Appu relaxed and asked, with excitement creeping into his tone, "How is she? I trust everything is going well."

"I bring you good news, Appu," the pastor replied. "She desires to join you and be a Christian."

"Praise God! You mean God has answered my prayers?" Then he added more thoughtfully, "But how do you know? I don't trust her father. He's a rascal. Maybe it's a trick. He must have heard. . . ."

"No, no, my brother!" He shook his head vigorously, then continued, "Kanama and Salome met your wife several times out in the woods. She says she believes in Jesus and desires to return home. She knew her father would object, preventing her meeting them again if he found out where she had been. In the event of her not coming, she asked us to bring you word."

He paused, then took a small package from his coat pocket. Handing it to Appu, he said, "This is from your wife. She told Kanama you would know what it means and act accordingly."

The gold bangle! Appu found it hard to control his emotions. He unwrapped it and held it close to his heart. Then he whispered, "Thank you, Jesus! Thank you!"

Gnanakan continued, "She desires to return to you with the children. But we heard rumors in the market that her father beat her and forbade her to leave the house. If it's true, this accounts for her absence from the meeting place in the woods."

"It must be true," remarked Appu. "He's that kind of person."

"Apparently the servants are talking," the pastor added. "It seems your wife is now treated as a widow. She wears cotton *saris*, and is forced to work in the kitchen. But by reports, she's very highly respected by the servants. I hear they're furious if anyone speaks against her. And," he laughed, "some say they're running a campaign in her favor!"

"Rukmoni!" Appu savored every word of her, as if tasting honey. He had missed his wife more than he could tell.

"What do you suggest, Pastor?" he asked impatiently.

"You'd like to go tonight, wouldn't you?" commented Ratnam chuckling.

"Yes, of course! Wouldn't you, if it was Padmini?" countered his friend.

"Not so hasty, brother," cautioned Pastor Gnanakan. "I think we had better ask the Lord's guidance so we don't make mistakes. It's crucial."

The men agreed. Then, after prayer, they seriously planned Rukmoni's rescue.

Chapter Sixteen
Rukmoni Returns

"So you're going to stay with the white *amma*, Raju?" asked Pastor Gnanakan of the little boy who held Mary's hand. Raju looked up and smiled. "I'll hear lots of stories now," he remarked. His mother looked out from the covered oxcart and gave last-minute instructions. "Don't forget to brush your teeth, and. . . ." The boy dashed forward and hugged her, then turned back to Peter and Mary. Padmini settled herself comfortably on the straw mattress for her eight-hour journey.

With a prayer, the rescue party was on its way, Appu and Ratnam walking with the other two men. For Padmini, this whole experience opened up a new world, since she had never before traveled beyond her own village.

By mid-afternoon they reached the pastor's home. He sent his son to call Kanama and Salome, and their report verified Appu's surmisings. Now Appu felt restless. Even though he anticipated trouble ahead, he longed to see his wife and children. He must go! Ratnam and Padmini pulled themselves away from the fellowship and joined him in his search.

As Appu's cart approached the bazaar, one of the servants recognized him and ran home to alert the family. "Your husband's coming," he quietly told Rukmoni. "Really?" she asked intently. "You wouldn't deceive me, would you?"

"Never, *amma*! I saw him with another man, and a lady riding in your master's oxcart."

"Thank you for letting me know," she whispered. "Have you told my parents?"

"Should I?" he asked. "I'll do whatever you say."

"Yes," she replied, "I think they should know."

With the cart moving slowly through the village, Rukmoni's

parents had ample time to prepare for the confrontation. Rukmoni continued to work in the kitchen, although she longed to pack her belongings and escape. But, she reflected, the Lord Jesus brought Appu! He would also release her to return home with her husband.

Rukmoni's parents were not the only ones who learned of Appu's approach. Neighbors and friends gathered from the entire area, anticipating a conflict.

"Just as well," commented Ratnam to his friend. "We need witnesses in the event her parents refuse to give up their daughter."

The cart stopped near Rukmoni's ancestral home. Appu moved toward the house. Suddenly his father-in-law came rushing out, livid with rage, flourishing his stick.

"Don't you dare take another step forward, or I'll kill you!" he shouted. "Get out of here, you . . . you . . . you. . . ." He faltered for words.

Appu spoke up, loud and clear. "Sir, I have come to see my wife and children. Will you send them to me?"

Meanwhile, Rukmoni's mother had firmly closed the door to the kitchen to prevent her daughter from knowing about her husband's appearance. The woman came onto the verandah and shouted to Appu, "My daughter refuses to see you or have anything to do with you. You have disgraced the family!"

"I don't think that is true," objected Appu firmly. "In any case, she is an adult and can speak for herself. I will hear what she has to say from her own lips. She is my wife, and I have a right to see her. If you refuse, I will seek legal justice. Let her speak for herself."

A murmur of approval rose from the crowd. Clearly, they were supporting Appu. But Appu's father-in-law wouldn't give up yet.

"You'd better get out of here fast," he yelled. "The whole village will be after you, you outcaste!"

A voice rose from the crowd. "That's not true! Appu speaks the truth! Send for your daughter. She is his wife!"

Sensing he was losing this battle, Rukmoni's father sent his wife indoors to call their daughter. Meanwhile, the servants had been telling Rukmoni what was happening. She quickly lifted her heart in prayer, that she would say and do the right thing, regardless of consequence. One thing she knew—she belonged to the Lord Jesus, and to Appu.

As mother and daughter neared the front door together, she heard the older woman say, "Don't you dare go with that man! Renounce him!" But the girl rushed out of the house and fell at her husband's feet.

Appu gently lifted her up. "You don't need to observe Hindu customs anymore, my love," he said quietly. "Now both of us belong to Jesus! We'll bow at His feet together."

From the crowd of onlookers came the voice again, "Appu, ask her. Will she go?"

"It's up to you to say, my dear," Appu said. "Go and tell your parents your decision. Have you decided?"

She nodded her head yes, looking down demurely. He continued, "Then tell your parents, loudly enough so that all these people can hear. Then they will know the truth." He made a broad sweep with his arm to include the witnesses.

The girl walked up to the verandah. In a loud, clear voice, she said, "Appu is my husband. I left him because he became a Christian. But about a month ago I saw the Lord Jesus in a vision, and I decided to follow Him." She paused for effect, then said firmly, "Now I want to go to live with my husband, and we will take our children. We will be Christians together."

There was no mistaking her decision. A murmur of approval went through the crowd. Her parents, speechless with anger, knew they were defeated. They turned away and shuffled into the house.

"Let me help you, *Amma*," said one servant after another. They called the children, helped pack all of Rukmoni's belongings, and escorted her out.

When Prem Kumar saw his father, he ran, shouting, "*Appa! Appa!* Are we going home with you? Please, *Appa*, take us home!"

"Yes, my son, you're coming with me. Now stay with your Uncle Ratnam while I help with the luggage." Ratnam put a protective arm around the lad and gave him a big smile.

Rukmoni handed her daughter, Premila, to Padmini. Then she turned back to say farewell to her parents. They had come onto the verandah again, but when she approached, they turned their backs. The crowd watched the entire proceedings and cheered as she respectfully folded her hands and spoke kindly to them. "I love you both," she said clearly, "and I will always be ready to help you."

Prem Kumar came running back. "I'm going home with *Appa*," he shouted with glee. "Goodbye, Big *Appa* and *Amma*." But their faces were cold and unyielding.

Appu came forward to bid farewell. They slammed the door in his face, and a murmur of disapproval went through the crowd. Appu turned back slowly, lifted his wife and child into the cart with Padmini and followed with Ratnam on foot.

But some of the servants ran after the cart. "Master," they said, "we're glad you came for *amma*! We love her, and any time you need help, just let us know. We'll come!"

Appu straightened his shoulders and took a deep breath. "Thank you! Thank you! You've made it easier for me. God bless you."

As the crowd melted away, Ratnam remarked, "Appu, that was hard! But the Lord gets the glory. Your wife gave a magnificent testimony. All heaven must be rejoicing!"

Appu's eyes shone. In light of that which he had gained, the rejection of Rukmoni's parents seemed very insignificant.

Inside the cart, Rukmoni turned to Padmini and said impulsively, "My sister, can you forgive me for treating you so badly?" She received a hug as her answer. Then followed confidences about what Jesus had done for each of them. They knew a bonding never before experienced, and it was sweet!

When the party arrived at Gnanakan's, everybody rejoiced. Rukmoni told of being beaten, her vision of Jesus, and the persecution alleviated by the loyalty of the servants. Her hearers listened with empathy; most of them had experienced similar rejections for their faith.

"You must stay," said Pastor Gnanakan's wife. "You need a rest, and the fellowship will do you good."

Since Appu thought Sundar could manage the shop for several days longer and Ratnam didn't have any pressing work in the fields, they waited. Special meetings would begin the next day with a missionary guest speaker, the pastor informed them.

Next morning, news spread that the missionaries' oxcart had been sighted near the village. Immediately, all the Christians formed a procession, carrying garlands and singing their welcome to the guests.

It was all new to Appu and Rukmoni! With Ratnam and Padmini at their side, they experienced a fellowship never known before. Kanama and Salome hovered over the group, seeing that their every need was met. Rukmoni learned of the intercession which effectively brought her and the children once more into freedom, and she rejoiced.

Perhaps the outstanding value of those several days was the bonding which these new believers felt with a larger body. They heard of new churches, new schools, and thrilled to learn that they weren't alone. Indeed, they had entered into a worldwide body, the Church of Jesus Christ.

Chapter Seventeen

Ratnam's Triumph

Ratnam watched the speaker intently, but his mind wandered. He saw himself as priest, pouring milk into a golden bowl. He had set that vessel before the temple cobra for years as his daily act of worship! Moreover, he believed so deeply in the cobra's deity that he taught his people to do the same.

In his reverie, the former priest visualized the scene: Puturaj, Siromani, Manickam, Dassan, and a host of others coming with their offerings of milk, marigolds, and money. They bowed, and they gave, as sincere acts of worship!

Who was responsible? Ratnam would have hidden if he could, but the Spirit of God seemed to say, "My child, I led you into the light. What about those whom you have left in darkness?"

With a start Ratnam sat upright to hear the preacher read, "You shall have no other gods before me."

The former priest bowed his head in shame. He struggled to find the answer to the big question, "How can I set the record straight?"

Not that he hadn't faced this issue before. Ratnam often resolved to witness to his neighbors in whatever way possible. However, he shrank from causing trouble for the growing community of new believers, and tried to maintain peace with non-Christians.

The speaker's words again penetrated his thoughts: "God has brought you into the light, my brother, my sister. Oh, yes! And don't we enjoy this fellowship? I do, and I'm sure you do, too! To sing and pray together, to share what God has done for each one of us is good. We need it. But . . ." he paused, pointing

73

emphatically at the crowd, "but, brother, what are you doing to bring light to your community?

"Suppose your neighbor's house caught on fire? Would you rush to his aid? I'm sure you would. I believe we'd all come with our buckets, and risk our lives to put out the fire which threatens our neighbor's life. Is his spiritual need of any less concern?

"I ask you to consider this matter. What is the bucket in your hand? God has ordered that He alone is to be worshipped. Yet, around us, our Hindu neighbors and friends are bowing to idols, the work of human hands. Some worship the sun, moon, and stars. Others deify animals, bowing to the cow, the snake, the monkey! But whatever form idolatry takes, all are in danger of hell fire. God's Word says so! Do you care? Will you do something?"

The preacher stepped back, moved with emotion, and whispered, "Come, friends, come and make a new commitment to the Lord. Show Him you care."

A solemn hush settled over the audience. One by one, people came forward as a token of total surrender to the Lord Jesus Christ. Although Ratnam remained in his seat, he knew he could never rest until he faced this challenge and answered it.

The guests prepared to leave after that concluding meeting. Ratnam and Padmini, along with Appu and his family, said goodbye to Pastor Gnanakan and their new friends and returned home.

The tall mission supervisor walked through the following days with a constant question in his heart: "My child, I led you into the light. What about those whom you have left in darkness?"

———

For the most part, the Christians now lived in peace with their Hindu neighbors. Ratnam, as mission supervisor, held the respect of the village even as he had as their former spiritual head. True, they heard reports of occasional stone-throwing, or beatings, and Pastor Gnanakan's people suffered constant insults. Appu learned that Kanama and Salome had gone to witness in the marketplace near Rukmoni's home. They had been chased by thugs whom the pastor suspected were incited by her father.

With comparative quiet in their bazaar, Ratnam easily could have suppressed the stirrings within concerning his responsibility to the village. But God's Spirit prodded him to action. Little things brought him face to face with the question. A woman bearing a tray of offerings for the cobra; Manickam, with a sneer, berating a debtor; Peter, with that slight accent and white face which marked him as a foreigner—ah, yes, little things! But oh, so weighty in the sight of God!

One day Ratnam faced the matter squarely. It was the slack time of the year in the fields. The tall man determined to visit every home in the village. He must give his personal testimony to all. Perhaps some wouldn't listen. No matter! This was the only way he would know inner freedom.

His witness tour occupied a full month. The former priest went from house to house. Where he was welcomed, he entered and enjoyed the hospitality offered. But such places were few. Most of the villagers feared breaking caste and offered Ratnam a seat under a nearby tree. Occasionally, as with Manickam and Dassan, he received harsh treatment—verbal insults, and even cow dung thrown at him. But the Christian took it calmly, reminding himself that the Lord Jesus suffered infinitely more to bring salvation.

Ratnam hoped that his witness tour would begin a chain reaction of villagers listening to the Christian message and accepting its truth. Sometimes, however, he knew deep discouragement.

Then came the night he visited Puturaj. The wizened old man opened the door slightly and looked out. "Yes?" he said. Seeing Ratnam, he observed, "What now, my friend? I hear you have become a fanatic."

"Why so?" inquired Ratnam with a big smile. He sensed warmth under the banter and noticed Puturaj pushing the door open a bit. "Come," invited the village elder.

Ratnam slipped in, and his friend quickly closed the door. Puturaj knew well the value of privacy, though one could never guarantee freedom from prying ears and eyes in such a public spot as this!

"Yes, yes," the village elder said, nodding, "I've heard about this business of your going from house to house. I wondered when it would be my turn, Ratnam." He rubbed his hands in satisfaction, then offered his guest a seat. "Wait," he said, "until I tell my wife to make coffee." He turned to the door, pulled aside the curtain and called, "Coffee for two, please, with snacks."

Ratnam's eyes followed him with interest. Unusual behavior, he thought. Has Puturaj calculated the extent of this risk? He's shrewd enough to know, most surely. The Christian raised a swift prayer, "Lord, I think you have prepared a heart for me here. Please give me the right words."

Rejoining his friend, Puturaj drew his seat closer and said, "Ratnam, I'm curious to know why you did it. Why did you leave your position as village priest to espouse a foreign religion? You know you became an outcaste!"

He chuckled, then continued, "Come to think of it, I've just taken an untouchable into my home, and we'll eat together! Your reason had better be worth it, friend. The price is terribly high!"

Ratnam smiled. "Puturaj, my brother, I want to thank you. I was pretty discouraged, and you have lifted my spirits. I'm not welcomed in most places."

"Then why do you do it?" questioned the old man, rubbing his bald head.

Ratnam leaned toward him and responded seriously, "Suppose your house was on fire, Puturaj. Wouldn't you want someone to come and help you put it out?"

"Of course, but what does that have to do with what I asked?"

The Christian pulled his Testament from his pocket. "Plenty," he replied. "I was ignorant before, worshipping the cobra. I taught all of you to do the same. Then God's Word reached me in my darkness. See what I found?" He opened the book and said, "My house was on fire! The white man came with his bucket and helped to extinguish it. I am grateful to him!"

"What fire?" asked the wizened villager.

"See here?" The two men pored over the Scriptures, hardly taking time to eat the tasty snack prepared by Puturaj's wife.

Ratnam returned home late that night, his heart filled with joy. Even though the village elder asked for more time to consider the Christian message, Ratnam sensed spiritual victory, and rejoiced. Several weeks later, Puturaj and his family declared their faith in Jesus. The village shook with the news.

Chapter Eighteen
Out of the Cobra's Clutches

"Now, Ratnam, can you rest?" asked Padmini of her husband. "See? You have visited every home, and the Lord is bringing people to Himself."

He nodded, yet the restlessness remained. True, he had met his people on a one-to-one basis and shared his testimony whenever possible. But many still worshipped the cobra as god. Daily, it slithered in and out to drink the milk they offered. It held them in fear.

"Lord Jesus," Ratnam agonized. "I am responsible. What more can I do?"

One morning he approached the missionary. "Peter," he said, "May I borrow your shotgun? I need it."

Peter looked up from his desk in the office. Since he was very busy, he didn't question Ratnam, supposing that he needed it to protect the fields from small game.

"Of course, Ratnam," he answered with a smile. "It's in the cupboard. Here's the key. Simply put it back when you're finished."

Peter returned to his work, scarcely giving the matter a second thought, while Ratnam got the gun.

He decided to wait until after lunch when Raju would return from school. Not many people stirred during the heat of the day. Early afternoon would be a good hour.

Raju and his father walked toward the cool woods. The boy was excited at the prospect of a hunt. He glanced at Ratnam and tried to match his stride.

Suddenly, Ratnam made a sharp turn and headed toward the village. "*Appa!*" cried the lad. "Where are we going? To the temple?"

"Yes, son," Ratnam replied seriously. "Come quickly."

They stopped at the entrance of the shrine. Ratnam surveyed the village. Nobody around? That's good, he thought. Raju saw the strained expression on his father's face and became alarmed. "*Appa!*" he cried.

The former priest stooped to look inside, adjusting his eyes to the dim light. Yes, the well-fed cobra lay coiled in the center of the dirt floor.

Ratnam faced his son. Putting his hand on the boy's shoulder, he looked deep into his eyes. "Raju," he said, "we have a job to do. I need your help. Go in and shoo the cobra out. You know how."

The boy pulled back. Noting his fear, Raju's father continued, "Be brave, my son. We're doing this for Jesus, and He's with us. Don't be afraid."

Raju straightened. Then, stooping, he peered into the darkness. Slowly he worked his way to where he could reach the plate on the shelf. He began thumping it on the ground.

The cobra stirred. It was used to this vibration which preceded the offering of milk. The lethargic reptile slithered out of the temple with head erect and hood flared. Menacingly, it glared at the priest who had so often come to worship there.

Ratnam took careful aim. The gun followed the slow, writhing motion of the snake. His hand trembled slightly, but then became firm with resolve. Now! Ratnam pulled the trigger.

The blast nearly deafened Raju, but he ran out in time to see the huge creature thrashing about. Then it lay still . . . dead!

People came running from everywhere. Amidst great confusion, some hurled abuse at Ratnam while others bowed before the serpent, crying. A few, secretly assenting to the gospel, admired Ratnam's courage.

Their former priest drew himself to full height and spoke. "My people," he said, "I am still your friend. I had to do this today because I am responsible for your darkness. I taught you to worship the cobra! I thought he was God. I was sincerely ignorant of the truth."

Everyone listened attentively as the man continued, "The day came when the Word of the true and living God came into my hands. I read for myself and found out I would die unless I changed. Now I realize that all of you will die unless you, too, come to the true and living God. This snake is not God!" He waved his hand toward the serpent. "Look at him," he cried. "He lies dead from a bullet wound! Will he rise from the dead, as did Jesus? No! My brothers and sisters, it is Jesus Christ who gives life!"

He stopped, looked at those earnest faces, and concluded simply, "Many of you may hate me for what I have done today, but I had to do it to clear my conscience. I taught you to worship the cobra. Now I will teach you a better way. I have killed him. Go give your milk to your babies, and buy food with your money."

Emotionally spent, Ratnam turned and walked steadily through the crowd in the direction of the mission. Earlier, Raju had run home in fear to tell Padmini of the incident. Peter also had heard the shot and started for the temple, but Arputham stopped him with arms outstretched. "No, master," he had cried. "You must not be seen there. Uncle Ratnam will come and tell you about it. You're safer here."

Peter turned back to the house, and soon Ratnam joined him.

"What have you done?" The missionary looked deep into his companion's eyes. "Tell me, Ratnam."

The tall man handed the gun to the white man. "I had to do it. . . . The cobra is dead!" he said grimly.

"The cobra? The cobra!" Peter stepped back and looked at the former priest. "Why, Ratnam?" he whispered in amazement. "Why take such a risk?" He put his arm around him as the man stood silent. Then he heard, "Peter, I had to do it. Now my conscience is clear."

"I know, my brother. But this could lead to more trouble. Don't you see? You are so impetuous, but so true, Ratnam."

"Thank you, Peter. Yes, trouble may come, but this wasn't a sudden decision. Nobody, not even Appu, understood. I was their priest, and I taught my people to worship that serpent. How then could I help them out of their bondage?" He drew a deep breath and concluded, "They may kill me for my faith in Jesus, but I didn't dare let that cobra live longer than I!"

Two days later Appu prepared to close his shop for the night. An inner voice spoke, "Take all your money, and as many valuables as you can carry. But don't empty your shop, or cause alarm."

Appu had learned to obey that inner voice, for the Lord often spoke to him. The shopkeeper quickly emptied his money box. He gathered a few valuables and handed them to his manager. Special customers often came to the master's house on business, so Sundar took them as a matter of course. Appu filled a bag with provisions, locked the shop, and the two men walked off together.

Near midnight, Appu and Rukmoni awakened to insistent knocking and shouting. "Appu! Appu! Your shop's on fire! Come, Appu!"

The man rushed to the scene to see flames licking doorways and windows. Soon the thatch roof caught fire, and the whole building became a blazing inferno. People poured out of houses, carrying buckets to put out the fire with water from a nearby well.

They formed a line, passing filled buckets from one to the next. In the glare Appu recognized people whom he had befriended in the past. Their willingness to help warmed his heart.

Suddenly, out of the darkness, Ratnam ran up to him. He threw his arms around Appu. "My brother," he cried, "I'm sorry! I've caused this! They're taking revenge on you. They're angry because I killed the cobra. I'm sorry." He could say no more.

Appu gripped his hand. "No, no, brother. Don't worry. You led me to the light, Ratnam. We'll share together, and the Lord will provide."

"You don't mind losing everything?" Ratnam asked, amazed. The former priest lifted his head and looked on the scene with glowing eyes.

"No, my friend," Appu announced. "Not since I've been delivered out of the cobra's clutches!"

Allen and Leoda Buckwalter

For Allen and Leoda Buckwalter, missionaries to India for forty-one years, missions is a way of life.

Allen, twin to Amos, grew up in southern California and attended Beulah Academy and College, later known as Upland College. He married Leoda Smith, daughter of missionary parents, on September 3, 1936; and went on to graduate from Pasadena College the following year. After serving in a country pastorate for two years in Illinois, they were sent to India, land of Leoda's birth, and arrived there November 20, 1939.

Their tenure in India was divided into two main parts: twenty years in orphanage supervision, village evangelism, and church planting among Santals in village India; and twenty years in missionary radio with the Far East Broadcasting Associates of India under FEBC Radio International. Allen served as Director for India in Bangalore for nine years, and as Branch Manager in Delhi for eleven years. In their last year in India they ministered as voluntary assistants to the pastor of the Centenary Methodist Church in New Delhi.

During their residence in Bangalore they met Thangam, a brave woman who suffered much for her faith in Christ. She uses the pen name "Thangam" (gold) to cover her identity.

Though retired from overseas ministries since 1981, the Buckwalters remain active in the cause of missions, representing FEBC Radio International in the northeastern United States. They have visited India twice since turning the work over to Indian leadership and an entirely national staff.